25

Manon
Massenet

Geraldine Farrar as Manon, one of her most famous roles in a career at the Met. that spanned from 1906-1922. (Stuart-Liff Collection)

Preface

This series, published under the auspices of English National Opera and The Royal Opera, aims to prepare audiences to evaluate and enjoy opera performances. Each book contains the complete text, set out in the original language together with a current performing translation. The accompanying essays have been commissioned as general introductions to aspects of interest in each work. As many illustrations and musical examples as possible have been included because the sound and spectacle of opera are clearly central to any sympathetic appreciation of it. We hope that, as companions to the opera should be, they are well-informed, witty and attractive.

The Royal Opera is very grateful to The Baring Foundation for making possible the publication of this Guide to *Manon*.

Nicholas John
Series Editor

25

Manon

Massenet, Jules

Opera Guide Series Editor: Nicholas John

Published in association with
English National Opera and The Royal Opera
and assisted by a generous donation
from The Baring Foundation

John Calder · London
Riverrun Press · New York

First published in Great Britain, 1984 by
John Calder (Publishers) Ltd, 18 Brewer Street,
London W1R 4AS

and

First published in the U.S.A., 1984 by
Riverrun Press Inc,
175 Fifth Avenue
New York, NY 10010

BRITISH LIBRARY CATALOGUING IN PUBLICATION DATA
Massenet, Jules
  Manon.—(Opera guide; 25)
  1. Massenet, Jules. Manon
  2. Operas—Librettos
  I.Title   II. Meilhac, Henri   III. Gille, Phillipe
  IV. John, Nicholas   V. Series
  782.1′092′4   ML410.M41

LIBRARY OF CONGRESS CATALOGING IN PUBLICATION DATA
Massenet, Jules, 1842-1912
  [Manon. Libretto. English & French]
  Manon.

  (Opera guide; 25)
  Includes libretto in French by Henri Meilhac and Phillipe Gille, based on the novel
Manon Lescaut by the Abbé Prévost, with English translation.
  'Published in association with English National Opera and The Royal Opera.'
  Discography: p. 111
  Bibliography: p. 112
  Includes index.

  1. Operas—Librettos. 2. Massenet, Jules 1842-1912.
Manon. I. Meilhac, Henri, 1831-1897.   II. Gille, Phillipe, 1831-1901.
III. Prévost, abbé, 1697-1763. Manon Lescaut.   IV. Title.   V. Series.
  ML50.M415M32 1984   84-755667

  ISBN 0-7145-4041-2

SUBSIDISED BY THE
Arts Council
OF GREAT BRITAIN

John Calder (Publishers) Ltd, English National Opera and
The Royal Opera House, Covent Garden Ltd receive financial
assistance from the Arts Council of Great Britain. English
National Opera also receives financial assistance from the
Greater London Council.

Typeset in Plantin by Margaret Spooner Typesetting, Dorchester, Dorset.

Printed in Great Britain by The Alden Press, Oxford.

Contents

List of Illustrations

Massenet

Gérard Condé

Massenet was precision itself: 'It is an obsession of mine' he was to declare proudly to the director of the Opéra when congratulated on his punctuality. And indeed what is striking about his scores, or rather his manuscripts, is their precision and legibility in spite of a hand that trembled increasingly with age.

This meticulousness is most apparent in his notation of the vocal lines: while, until the beginning of the 20th century, it was traditionally desirable to leave the singer freedom of phrasing and accent, there is scarcely a note in the voice parts which Massenet has left unmarked as to dynamics, staccato or legato, without an accent or indication of expression, in order to fit the natural inflexions of French prosody closely and to make the text as comprehensible as possible. He also indicated metronome readings with the greatest precision and his metronome, inscribed with the titles of the scores for which it was used, is preserved. Is this in case someone should wish to check the exact tempo according to the composer's own metronome — which was perhaps capricious?

Anxious to see his musical thoughts executed without the slightest alteration, Massenet has left nothing that was not definitive. Almost without exception he did away with his sketches and early versions of certain pages so as to leave posterity only orchestral scores without second thoughts. There are several reasons for this clarity: firstly Massenet had obtained from his publisher a very thick paper which could be erased without damage and then, writing as he did only on loose leaves and only on the *recto*, it was little trouble for him to begin a page again if it had started badly, to interpolate one, to take one back or to change it with an afterthought. Lastly, like most opera composers of the 19th century, Massenet composed firstly a sort of piano/vocal reduction and only orchestrated it when the work had found its definitive form.

Although he taught composition at the Paris Conservatoire until 1896, Massenet dedicated his summer holidays to composition properly speaking and orchestrated during the winter, either at home or in hotels — wherever the supervision of the first performances of his works took him. In a sense it was desk work, routinely carried out as a rule, but occasionally relieved by feats of virtuosity such as the orchestration of the 257 pages of *La Navarraise* between November 30 and December 9 1893 ... This is not to say that Massenet had always found work easy: his first grand opera, *Le Roi de Lahore*, occupied him from 1872 to 1877 and the orchestration of *Manon* took him nearly five months to complete. Yet, with Massenet, a beginner's natural inexperience gave way to a solid craftsmanship perfectly suited to the ends he pursued; it assured him of a sort of technical infallibility even when inspiration, in the modern sense of the word, failed him.

Paradoxical as it may seem to those who are satisfied with the picture of a sentimental composer, an inexhaustible melodist, Massenet was the complete opposite of instinctive. He had little experience of composition when he won the Prix de Rome at the age of 22 and, as he gradually learnt his craft, he derived increasingly substantial inspiration from it. Once appointed professor of composition, at the age of 36, he only wrote model scores which lent

Marie Heilbronn and Jean-Alexandre Talazac who created the roles of Manon and Des Grieux (Stuart-Liff Collection)

themselves willingly to analysis. When his operas are examined from this angle, it might be said that Massenet approached each dramatic situation as a problem to solve: the musical solution is born from the acuteness of the analysis. Unfortunately the ease with which he found coherent musical solutions to artificial situations or badly constructed dramas must have forced him more than once to put up with clumsy librettos which ruined whole scores, or which are, at least, responsible for unsuccessful scenes and weak acts.

One cannot say that Massenet, from his infancy, had a particularly strong vocation to be a composer. Born in Montaud (near Saint-Etienne) in 1842, Massenet was the youngest of a family of twelve; he hated his first name so much that he would only tolerate the initial. He first trained as a pianist when his parents had moved to Paris and even performed several times as a soloist in 1858; in the following year he won first prize at the Paris Conservatoire. With his parents now installed at Chambéry, Massenet had to support his needs by accompanying singers or playing the triangle in the orchestra at the Gymnase, or the kettledrum at the Café Charles or the Théâtre Lyrique. Thus it was that he gained direct experience of the theatre: he was in the pit, for instance, at the première of Gounod's *Faust*.

He studied composition under Ambroise Thomas, and won the Prix de Rome in 1863. Four years later he owed his Opéra Comique debut to a new disposition instituted in favour of the prize-winners: although the 'curtain raiser' *La Grand-tante* enjoyed a certain success, it did not do much to open the doors of other theatres for him. He had to wait another five years before the withdrawal of a colleague saw him entrusted with the libretto of an opéra-comique, *Don César de Bazan*, for which he composed the music in record time. From this period date the *Overture* for *Phèdre* and the stage music for *Les Erinnyes*, both of which found immediate favour, but it was the production at the Odéon, in April 1873, of the oratorio *Marie-Magdeleine* which assured his true repute. Although remodelled, this youthful work had been completed several years before and is not only remarkable on account of the personal inspiration it demonstrates, but also because Massenet was not to rediscover this language — already so much his own — until *Manon*.

Eve (*Mystère en trois parties*), composed in the following year, 1874, enjoyed as lively a success but, apart from a few pages, it does not show notable progress. At the same time, having conceived *Les Templiers* and written a couple of acts which seemed to him to be too reminiscent of Meyerbeer, Massenet concentrated his efforts on a grand opera in five acts, *Le Roi de Lahore*. After the brilliant success of this opera, given at the Paris Opéra in April 1877, Massenet would have expected a warmer welcome from the new director when, in 1881, he proposed the first performance of *Hérodiade*[1]. But Vaucorbeil refused and, since he had several other operatic projects in mind (notably *Robert de France* and *Les Girondins*), it is understandable that Massenet eagerly accepted a proposal from Carvalho, the director of the Opéra Comique; for his part, Carvalho wished to see Henri Meilhac's *Phoebé* set to music and naturally turned to the most highly regarded of young composers.

Massenet had already collaborated with Meilhac on a small comic piece: *Bérangère et Anatole* was given at the Cercle de l'Union Artistique in February 1876 but the composer, heedful of his reputation as a serious musician, has let nothing survive from it. It is probable that the subject of *Phoebé* did not correspond to his current aspirations because he later returned

---

[1] It was eventually produced in Brussels in 1883.

9

Massenet's own
favourite photograph
of himself
(Stuart-Liff Collection)

the libretto to Meilhac and, opéra-comique for opéra-comique, Massenet replied by proposing *Manon* after the celebrated book by the abbé Prévost. As early as the following day, if *Mes souvenirs* are to be believed (although they were not actually collected by Massenet), Meilhac had made out the outline of the first two acts; the others followed shortly afterwards. But the libretto only reached its definitive form as the opera was composed, between May and October 1882. Massenet made frequent and fruitful visits to his librettist (who had a collaborator in Philippe Gille); he himself suggested the scene in Saint-Sulpice and, most importantly, obtained a text that suited his own ideas — for, while he accepted opéra-comique in principle, he had no intention of following the conventions of a genre that was exhausted dramatically.

When Massenet presented his score in the autumn of 1883 it had already been engraved so as to prevent any alterations: Carvalho was notorious for his mania for 'remodelling' the works he produced. Besides, Massenet had premonitions about the cuts that people would be tempted to make in order to condense the action or to place Manon and Des Grieux systematically in the foreground. Such cuts entirely destroy the overlapping effect desired by the authors and the contrast between the personal drama and the general rejoicing[2].

[2] Some time after the first performance, Massenet himself made some changes to the score. Firstly for the sake of Sybil Sanderson: the Bibliothèque de l'Opéra de Paris possesses a copy of the original version with the composer's manuscript alterations of details. Then Massenet introduced a Gavotte ('Obéissons quand leur voix appelle') for the prima donna Marie-Roze; and then, for the sake of Mme. Bréjeau-Silver, he proposed that a *Fabliau* with more virtuoso vocal writing should replace the Gavotte.

The original set for Act One at the Opéra-Comique in 1884 (Stuart-Liff Collection)

With *Le Cid* (1884-1885), Massenet again demonstrated that the demands of grand opera inspired him above all to write formulas, if not commonplaces. Although the subject of *Werther* (1885-1887) at first seems to have excited him less than *Le Cid*, it offered him an intimate setting in which he could better rediscover his creative powers. Created in Vienna in 1892, in German, *Werther* was given in Paris in 1893 with limited success. The chromaticism of the new work might lead one to think that Massenet, who had been at Bayreuth in 1886, had been influenced by the composer of *Tristan*; to be precise, however, Massenet had by then been an informed admirer of Wagner for almost thirty years. The Wagnerian model was much stronger — too strong perhaps — in *Esclarmonde* (1887-1888); the performances, which took place in the context of the Exposition Universelle, enjoyed a considerable success which reflected on Sybil Sanderson, for whom Massenet wrote the title role. In comparison with the preceding works, there is a noticeable expansion of the melodic line, but the dramatic action does not maintain the same intensity up to the end.

In *Le Mage* (1889) Massenet fell again into the trap of grand opera, which the complexity of the plot further worsened. It was well received but the work was not revived. The same year saw the composition of *Amadis*, a legendary opera which, through a combination of circumstances, was not produced until after his death. It was reworked in 1910 and first performed in 1922 in Monte Carlo (as were the majority of his operas after 1900). The work may be uneven but it has the distinction of a prologue which contains writing of an audacious

11

nature that Massenet never otherwise essayed — a combination of archaism and modernity, as in the late works of Liszt.

Intended for the Opéra Comique, *Thaïs* was first given at the Opéra in 1894; this fact throws a misleading perspective on a work of a rather intimate character which mixes the sacred and the sensual, the serious and the comic, in a way that is no doubt surprising — but entirely original. His next opera, *La Navarraise*, first performed in London in 1894, is so resolutely tragic in tone,

2nd Act: Duo of the letter   3rd Act Manon & Des Grieux in St Sulpice

4th Act: In the gambling house, Des Grieux & his father

however, that it has been seen as a concession, or a conversion, to the *verismo* then fashionable in Italy. In fact, the influence worked both ways. From 1893 to 1901 Massenet returned several times to *Griselidis*, of which he made several versions; here, as in *Thaïs*, he was attempting a fusion of styles but the musician's faith in the libretto was misplaced. As though intent on making an inventory of the resources of his imagination, Massenet then entered the world of fairy stories with *Cendrillon* (1894-1895) and demonstrated a true genius for his craft, which makes the feebleness of his libretto all the more regrettable.

On the death of Ambroise Thomas, Massenet was offered the directorship of the Conservatoire but he refused and indeed, increasingly preoccupied with his career and the travel it involved, he also resigned as professor of

3rd Act: Manon at the promenade, 'Cours la Reine'

Illustrations from 'The Graphic' of the first London production at Drury Lane in 1885 (Royal Opera House Archives)

composition. Varied as his pupils were, they all acknowledged his pedagogic judgement. He was a born teacher, and did not stifle their individual differences; through their works they bear witness to the solid instruction he gave them. Among them were Alfred Bruneau, Gabriel Pierné, Xavier Leroux, Gustave Charpentier, Henri Rabaud, Charles Koechlin, Florent Schmitt — all Prix de Rome pize-winners — and Ernest Chausson, Guy Ropartz and Reynaldo Hahn who did not try for it.

The first fruit of the complete freedom that Massenet now enjoyed was *Sapho*, to which he devoted the summer of 1896. It is not known what stimulated him, since he was not exactly religious, to adapt the *Vulgate* himself for an oratorio, *Terre promise*, at which he worked between 1897 and 1899. The fable of *Le Jongleur de Notre Dame*, by contrast, corresponded better to his personal beliefs; throughout this work, and quite apart from the author's own poetic vision, the revival of interest in Gregorian chant and medieval music which was then taking place is apparent. Contemporary with *Le Jongleur*, the Piano Concerto was first performed in 1902; old sketches were very probably re-used in the finale but the *adagio* is typical of the autumnal harmonic colour which characterises Massenet's late style.

5th Act: Lescaut bribing the Sergeant

5th Act: Death of Manon

Cobalet as the Count Des Grieux and Taskin as Lescaut, creators of the roles in Paris, 1884 (Stuart-Liff Collection)

At the same time he undertook *Roma*, beginning an 'antique' period which would include *Ariane* (1905), *Bacchus* (1907-1908), *Roma* (1902-1910) and *Cléopatre* (1911-1912). In these pieces the workmanship is irreproachable and the inspiration is less absent than is generally believed; they enjoyed only a very limited success. While *Chérubin*, written in a few days, is evidence of the composer's virtuosity, more than anything else, *Thérèse* (1905-1906), a story of the Revolution, as intense as *Chérubin* was light, offers additional proof of his capacity to renew himself. While *Panurge* (1910-1911) 'haulte farce en musique', has left no trace, *Don Quichotte* (1908-1909), created by Chaliapin, may be numbered among his four or five unarguable successes.

In spite of declining health on account of cancer, Massenet's activity did not slow up until his death in Paris on August 13, 1912. The date August 14 is inscribed on his tomb at Egreville because the composer had not written the number 13 for years. Indeed, after the composition of *Le Cid* (1884), he adopted the habit of systematically replacing the figure 13 by 12A in his pagination. As a last precaution, in the score of *Panurge* he passed directly from page 12 to page 14..

On the day after his death the musical world extolled the memory of the composer of *Manon* as though that was his only claim to glory. Yet it is true that from the first it was this work — just twenty-one years after its creation it had celebrated its 500th performance at the Opéra-Comique — which had enjoyed a popularity that none of the twenty operas Massenet wrote later could challenge. A quote from *Manon* in the mouth of one of the Montmartre seamstresses in the second act of Gustave Charpentier's *Louise* attests in its way to the popularity among all classes of the opera around 1900. It is no less significant that, in 1892-93, Massenet agreed to write *Le Portrait de Manon* (an act in the purest opéra-comique style), a sort of sequel which might be thought — although there is no proof — to be intended to make amends to the director of the Opéra Comique for the loss of his principal Manon, Sybil Sanderson, who was now engaged by the Opéra, where she would create *Thaïs*. *Manon* is a mature work, less ambitious than those which surround it (*Hérodiade, Le Cid*) yet more crafted and perfect than many which followed. It is in many ways pastiche, or imitation, opéra-comique and owes a part of its artistic success to the fact that it is more an exercise in style — a sequence of genre pictures — than a sentimental drama. In fact it is more notable for its pastiche than for its lyrical effusions, and Massenet found in it both a stimulus for his technical skill and the opportunity to treat the love duets without exaggeration. One cannot say that performers have always followed him in this respect, but the stature of masterpieces may be measured by their capacity to survive such misinterpretation.

Fanny Heldy, who made her debut at Covent Garden as Manon in 1926 (Stuart-Liff Collection)

15

John Treleaven as Des Grieux with Valerie Masterson as Manon and Niall Murray as Lescaut at ENO, 1980 (photo: Andrew March)

A Musical Synopsis

Hugh Macdonald

Manon is entitled 'opéra-comique', a term which in 1883 no longer implied that the plot would be light-hearted and that all would turn out well. After Bizet's *Carmen* in 1875 no subject could seem too strong for the genre and Manon's distressing end on the road to Le Havre was certainly not too extreme. There did not even have to be a comic element, although *Manon* contains many scenes and characters that belong wholly to the lighter tradition. Massenet's particular skill was his sure sense of theatrical timing and movement; the contrast of passion and pleasure which is so much part of Prévost's novel is a vital aspect of the opera. The contrasts between acts, as much as those between scenes, afford opportunities for all kinds of colourful settings and characters to throw a straightforward but tragic love story into relief.

Perhaps the only surviving requirement of opéra-comique was the spoken dialogue which survives in *Manon* as the frequent use of speech over music. This can throw a *frisson* into the action in such scenes as the arrival of the police in Act Four, or, following the old German tradition of *Melodram*, intensify the expressive weight of an emotional scene, as when the lovers' main theme [9] is first heard. Alternatively it can hasten along the action when musical elaboration would be out of place, as when the innkeeper goes about his business in Act One. Every character has lines to speak at some point, and speech is used for comic relief as well as emotional tension. There is never any feeling of experiment on these occasions, for Massenet's judgement in such matters was impeccable.

He was able to incorporate all the varity of scenes and settings that French opera traditionally exploited and which his audiences adored: a church scene, a gambling scene, a street scene, for example, all offering opportunities for choral participation and lively movement. A ballet is worked dexterously into the action in Act Three, Scene One. One of the richest sources of colour in *Manon* is the evocation of 18th-century France with recurrent baroque stylisations many of them nearer to an original style than we might expect of a composer of that time. Rameau and the claveçinistes offered an idiom which worked particularly well in Act Three, Scene One, for both chorus and ballet. If time and place could be effectively suggested by this pastiche music, passion is the domain of the modern style, its force all the more powerful for its proximity with a faintly nostalgic lost world. We are reminded perhaps of Tchaikovsky's *The Queen of Spades* or Delibes's *Le roi s'amuse*, both composed later than *Manon*. The French had just started to reprint scores of their earlier masters — Lully, Rameau and others — in a burst of national pride, and a neo-classical craze was under way.

Prévost's novel was a happy choice not only because of its historical setting but also for its atmosphere and affecting subject. Gounod was Massenet's most prominent model in general dramaturgy and style, although the novel had been set (very disappointingly) by Auber in 1856 without any of the reality of emotional exchanges to which Massenet responded so avidly, for in this respect he surpassed even Gounod with a

17

much more acute sense of theatre and a more penetrating sympathy for human feeling. Perhaps Massenet had learned a little from Bizet's paramount genius in *Carmen*, perhaps quite a lot from Verdi, not forgetting the similarity of Verdi's père Germont in *La Traviata* and Massenet's Comte des Grieux, striking enough in dramatic effect even without the curious intervention of both fathers in gambling scenes in both operas. But Massenet's gifts seem so natural and his feeling for voices so instinctive that it would be unfair to pilfer any credit that is properly his due.

Of course like all advanced composers in the later 19th-century he was accused of borrowing from Wagner, and a fully developed set of leitmotifs seemed to confirm the charge. He scarcely needed to refute it, though, since the attachment of motifs to ideas was a well-established operatic principle long before Wagner hijacked it; it was a natural outcome of the universal belief that music in opera must reflect the mood, character and meaning of the libretto. If Wagner had never existed Masssenet would have composed the same *Manon* with the same motifs functioning in the same way. It is not drily systematic, and can occasionally be puzzling, but he gives most of his characters distinctive motifs that mark their entrances and actions. Lescaut has two motifs, Brétigny and Guillot have one each. Manon has two which both pass out of sight quite quickly, since she grows up with frightening rapidity: her innocent motifs [4] and [7] serve no purpose once that innocence is past. Motif [10] reflects her more playful self, but is not heard in the latter part of the work. Lescaut's motifs do not accompany his appearance in the last act, and the most powerful motif of the lovers' passion [9], despite being (or because it is) used recurrently throughout the opera, is passed over at the final curtain.

This motif technique overlaps with the standard 19th-century technique of identifying a scene, long or short, with an orchestral motif, heard

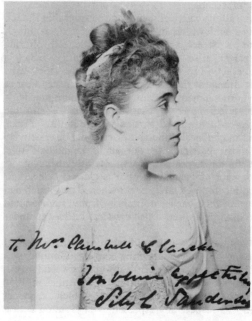

Sybil Sanderson,
who was the first to sing
the title role
at Covent Garden
in 1891
(Stuart-Liff Collection)

18

Marie Roze, the first exponent of the title role in London, Drury Lane, 1885
(BBC Hulton Picture Library)

intermittently throughout. The gambling motif [23] functions this way in Act Four and the soldiers' motif [25] in Act Five. Sometimes a motif is no more than the principal melody of an air, or piece, or *morceau*, whether solo or ensemble, binding that piece together, and it may or may not be later recalled, depending on dramatic necessity. Lescaut's song [17] is echoed later, the Comte's [20] is not. Massenet undoubtedly relished the great flexibility offered by the freedom to draw on earlier motifs and to use them as building material in later scenes, but he also understood the necessity and effect of new ideas introduced quite late in the drama when circumstances and characters have changed.

It is often thought to be unfair to Massenet to draw attention to the set-pieces in his operas, and although the trend was then all towards endless, seamless dramatic unfolding, neither Massenet nor Verdi ever lost sight of the *scena* as a self-contained operatic event. The score of *Manon* can easily be marked and indexed with the *morceaux* which are almost detachable (in that they begin and end in the same key and have clearly defined starts and finishes) and which bring forward one character (or more) to the centre of the stage. There are two examples in the first act: Manon's

19

opening song 'Je suis encor ... tout étourdie ...' ('I'm so confused ...') and Lescaut's morality on family pride 'Regardez-moi bien dans les yeux' ('Now then, look me straight in the eye!'). Sometimes these scenes are extended over a longer period with interruptions that almost conceal their residual functions as operatic set pieces.

While the motifs do define character in a recognizable way, Massenet uses many other means to build up characterisation, including the interplay of speech, recitative and full-blooded song and the delicate application of orchestral colours. In his love duets he relies too readily on the cliché of a powerful octave unison, though he was probably the first (anticipating Tchaikovsky and Puccini) to exploit the effect of a massive string unison against wind chords. *Manon* also has some remarkable examples of orchestral restraint, especially in Acts Two and Five. The atmosphere of the gaming tables has never been so cleverly evoked as in the pounding pizzicatos of Act Four. Des Grieux's complex characterisation explodes the belief that Massenet could only portray female characters with true feeling, and once Manon has been lured into the social world, it is difficult ever quite to believe in her attachment to Des Grieux as wholly as in his for her. Yet because Manon is the only female character (apart from the puppet-like trio of Poussette, Javotte and Rosette) against five males with various claims on her, she cannot fail to hold our attention when she is on stage. Her plight is no less touching because she appears, at times, both fickle and shallow. Massenet's sense of her impudence and gaiety makes this image of the Eternal Feminine perfectly sympathetic.

*

The Prelude makes no attempt to set a scene or tell a story but assembles some contrasting themes from the opera as a curtain-raiser. The first is the bustling gavotte [16] that opens the Cours-la-Reine scene in Act Three. A snatch of the guards' music in the last act [25] connects this to Des Grieux's luxuriant declaration of love ('Manon, sphinx étonnant') from Act Four; a notably imaginative effect in an otherwise perfunctory Prelude is achieved by letting the music revert back from D♭ to F, but leaving Des Grieux's line untransposed, as if it were still in D♭.

The courtyard of the inn at Amiens is full of bustle and action. Guillot de Morfontaine and Brétigny, two wealthy Parisians, are joined by the inseparable Poussette, Javotte and Rosette in hustling the inn-keeper, and their five voices make a superlative ensemble with touches of mock-fugue and brisk comedy. The inn-keeper's eventual appearance disarms them, and their meal is served. Theme [1] suggests the mock solemnity as the mouth-watering delicacies appear, rather like the similar scene in Strauss's *Bourgeois Gentilhomme*, and all retire to a pavilion to indulge themselves.

A crowd gathers in expectation of the coach from Arras on its way to Paris. The coach's theme [2] is always in the bass while the inn bell is sounded (in the orchestra) to announce its arrival. With a snatch of an 18th-century minuet the chorus confesses its curiosity to see who's travelling where. Lescaut arrives with two of his drinking and gambling companions and packs them off to a near-by inn while he waits for his cousin Manon (an alteration from Prévost's novel, where she is his sister). Once only in this scene do we hear Lescaut's first theme [3], with its suggestion of pomposity rather than resolution. The coach arrives ([2] with its bells) and the music breaks into a rapid scamper as all attend to their luggage. Theme [2] is

Enrico Caruso as Des Grieux in 1903 (Stuart-Liff Collection)

21

converted into a variant of the bell idea, and the full chorus bemoans the discomforts of travel.

Theme [4], introduced suddenly by the clarinet, marks the entrance of Manon. She is sixteen, irresistibly pretty, and still unsure of herself, as her theme suggests. Lescaut [3] presents himself and they embrace. Manon's aria is based on [4] with echoes of [2] when she describes her journey. As [4] moves to Db she confesses her susceptibility to all the new impressions of her journey, and then goes on to admit her capacity for sudden girlish laughter also, little knowing that frivolity is the fatal flaw in her character. After a reprise of the lively chorus (for no particular reason), they are left alone, and Lescaut goes in search of her luggage. The lecherous old Guillot de Morfontaine then emerges from the pavilion to order more wine and sees Manon. He at once makes a proposition which provokes Manon's laughter, not anger, while his companions summon him back [5]; his attempts to plan an elopement with her are accompanied by snatches of theme [1] which is henceforth attached more to Guillot than to the food he eats. He withdraws on the appearance of Lescaut who feels obliged to give Manon a precautionary talking-to, a set-piece in A major structured on a new theme [6] which also, like [3], suggests a firmness of character which he does not really possess. He appeals to their family honour.

Left alone once more, Manon reflects not on what she has just heard but on the prettiness and vivacity of Guillot's three mistresses in the pavilion [5]. Snatches of [4] give place to a set piece [7], in which she attempts to persuade herself that she has to devote herself to convent life and leave such fun and laughter behind. It is a touching solo, not without its moment of passionate resignation.

A young man comes in, thinking of his father and his home. His theme [8] reveals a serious and sensitive nature. It is the Chevalier Des Grieux. His first sight of Manon is described in a remarkable passage with a winding, angular line over thick, low chords: he senses at once that something momentous has happened to him. Although he is reduced to plain speech, the orchestra is already giving out their love theme [9] with undisguised passion, and a duet takes shape. Manon confesses her frailty with a touch of [7], Des Grieux's theme [8] glows with warmth and [9] seals a fatal and instantaneous magnetism. Theme [1] indicates the arrival of Guillot's postillion. Manon's impulsive mind seizes the idea of eloping with Des Grieux to Paris. Realism would demand an immediate departure, but operatic licence permits them a fanciful glimpse of a carefree life in Paris. Poussette, Javotte and Rosette are heard [5] in the pavilion, and this reminds Manon of the temptations of an indulgent life. To an agitated version of [9] Manon and Des Grieux hurry away, just before Lescaut [6], drunk and penniless, arrives. The final scene is based on theme [1], rounding off the act as Lescaut accuses Guillot of abducting Manon and the innkeeper reveals the truth. Guillot swears revenge.

Act Two, in Manon and Des Grieux's apartment in Paris, brings together his theme [8] with a new theme for her [10] suggesting her eternal lightness of spirit. There is a baleful contrast between the two, even though in musical terms they combine effectively. The reading of Des Grieux's letter to his father is cleverly managed. She reads 'On l'appelle Manon . . .' ('And they call her Manon') — in a melody which Des Grieux later takes up 'Comme l'oiseau qui suit . . .' ('She's like a bird in Spring') — in a higher key with horn and harp accompaniment before their voices merge. Over [9], they fall

Nellie Melba as Manon at Saint Sulpice in Act Three (Stuart-Liff Collection)

into speech, and over [10] a glimpse of jealousy intrudes. Lescaut ([3] and [6]) and Brétigny (disguised as a guardsman) enter, and their arrival leads quickly to an ensemble of tension and confusion [11], since Des Grieux is quite reasonably affronted by their intrusion. Lescaut lures him away to the window leaving Brétigny free to woo Manon, whose coquetry is now much more evident in her character than any fidelity she may have promised to Des Grieux. Brétigny's attentions are supported by a fervent theme [12] to which Manon readily responds. Lescaut and Brétigny depart like a comic couple, as if to belie the ardour of the latter's suit.

Mary Garden as Manon. She made her Covent Garden debut in the role in 1902. (Stuart-Liff Collection)

Theme [10] is tempered with simplicity as [13] while Des Grieux leaves to post his letter, but as soon as he is gone [12] reappears more passionately than ever as Manon yields to the temptations offered by Brétigny. Her celebrated monologue [14] is a moving farewell to their life together, her voice accompanied only by slow chords, thinly scored: a *tour de force* of restraint. When Des Grieux returns he starts with an outburst of [9] but then launches into a rhapsody about the simple country life [15] to the accompaniment of high, simple textures. Motifs associated with Lescaut and Brétigny are heard when a knock on the door heralds Des Grieux's treacherous removal by Brétigny's men. Manon has only a 'Mon pauvre chevalier!' to offer before [12] steals her away.

The first scene of Act Three is an outdoor scene, full of picturesque evocations of 18th-century street life. Theme [16] recurs frequently, interspersed with music from a dance-hall where Poussette and her friends are, as usual, enjoying themselves. Lescaut is in extravagant humour, having (one supposes) been winning for once. He sings a piece deriding thrift [17], with a middle section in praise of an imaginary Rosalinde in artificially baroque style. The company is well entertained, especially by his promises of generosity. Guillot and Brétigny converse over the dance music, and a new energy in the orchestra, with an obviously frivolous pendant [18], renews the outdoor bustle in some clever choral exchanges. Manon arrives, enjoying much admiration, and sings a piece in an unbalanced septuple pulse which gives her every opportunity to exhibit her beauty, her trills and her coloratura; although not in the original score, in a later version she continues with the enchanting gavotte 'Profitons bien de la jeunesse' ('In delay there lies no plenty').

The mood changes sharply with the arrival of the Comte Des Grieux, the Chevalier's father, especially when Manon overhears the news of her former lover's retreat to St Sulpice for the purpose of taking orders. The Comte's music is always dignified and touching, though he has no motif of his own. The act closes with a grand tableau occasioned by Guillot engaging a ballet to entertain Manon and thus, as he supposes, to upstage Brétigny. Manon's thoughts are elsewhere, however, and we are left to admire Massenet's felicitous reproduction of Rameau's style and orchestration and to enjoy, like all French audiences, the ballet.

Act Three Scene Two permits Massenet another regular standby of French opera, a church scene, using the organ and chant-like melody as a background to the highly charged reunion of Manon and Des Grieux. Soft chords on the organ precede some decorous imitative entries of theme [19]. Des Grieux's first sermon provokes the congregation's eager admiration as they leave the seminary chattering to almost alarmingly irreverent music. The Comte congratulates his son, as he reflects bitterly on his former life (an ironic memory of [9]). His father sings a fine piece based on [20], full of propriety and exhortation. Des Grieux, left alone, has a monologue [21] in which his inability to forget Manon becomes more and more overpowering. With consummate skill Massenet incorporates within Des Grieux's monologue the verger's brief interruption 'C'est l'office!', calling him to the service, so that the tolling bell at the end summons him away and rounds off the number. Manon arrives and an oboe gives out a fragment of [9], desolately bare of accompaniment. The off-stage Magnificat provides exactly the dramatic contrast for Manon's prayer imploring the return of Des Grieux's love.

Edmond Clément as Des Grieux. He was the leading tenor at the Opéra-Comique, Paris from 1889-1909 (Stuart-Liff Collection)

When he appears, an emotional scene is inevitable. Even as he asserts that he has put her from his mind an agitated version of [9] reveals that this is not so, and it eventually reaches its old rhythm in its old key, F, when she implores not heaven, now, but Des Grieux himself. She pleads in a piece of bewildering directness [22], supported by a solo violin. He yields, of course, to this cajolery; [9] is triumphant, and the curtain falls.

Act Four, like the first scene of Act Three, is dominated by its atmosphere, not this time an outdoor scene but a notorious gaming hall, the Hôtel de Transylvanie, and the superb restlessness of motif [23] evokes these shady surroundings at regular intervals. Lescaut is in his element and again in boisterous mood [17]. The card sharpers have a lively song and the trio Poussette, Javotte and Rosette are inevitably there too, though without their theme [5]. Lescaut sings a *morceau* in praise of the Queen of Spades. Guillot enters: his *morceau* is enigmatic and fragmentary, allowing the orchestra to indicate most of the gestures to fill out his vanity.

A disturbance is heard and [18] somewhat inappropriately announces the arrival of Des Grieux and Manon. He is wary and distressed, and confesses in a deeply-felt statement of [24] both his passion and his despair at her elusive and 'too feminine' taste for money and pleasures. He is lured to the table by Manon and her cousin, with a background of [23] and a return of [24] now built into a grand trio. Before the stakes are down Manon and the three girls sing (now, almost wearyingly) in praise of money; the piece has an upper G pedal which eventually turns into Manon's triumphant trill, ending on a high C. The gaming begins, [23] again, and Des Grieux wins from Guillot, generating a violent argument in which everyone joins. Manon begs Des Grieux to leave, but his honour forbids such a dishonourable departure when he has been accused of cheating. They are still there when a forceful knock announces the police. Acting on Guillot's instructions they have come to arrest Des Grieux and Manon, and the ensemble is completed by the stern and improbable appearance of his father. The final brief ensemble has a Verdian grandeur.

Massenet's final scene is set on the road to Le Havre, not as in Prévost's novel or Puccini's *Manon Lescaut* (1893), in the desert of Louisiana. Manon, condemned as a prostitute, is being escorted with other women prisoners; a snatch of melody which appears in the minor in the bass [25] or in the major in the treble, to be whistled by the soldiers, evokes recollections of *Carmen*. Its pendant (already heard in the Prelude) is reminiscent of Beethoven's *Les Adieux* sonata, whether intentional or not. The thinness of the textures in this scene not only evokes the desolation of the scene, it also looks forward strikingly to Britten's operatic technique. There is a certain irony in the recurrence of this playful motif as the tragedy is played out.

When Manon arrives a new figure [26] accompanies her plaintive dialogue with Des Grieux, and a powerful duet follows [27]. The hint of [9] contained within [26] makes it inevitable background when she begins to recall their first meeting and their life together. [27] and [9] break into her faltering phrases, and Des Grieux even tries to revive her with [22], the song with which she had saved him from taking orders. But this time it cannot save her. It grows to a great unison, but her strength fails. Her dying words 'Et c'est là . . . l'histoire . . . de Manon Lescaut!' ('So now you know the story of Manon Lescaut') bring back a distant snatch of [7], recalling more innocent days, before [22] brings down the curtain.

Geneviève Vix as Manon at the Opéra-Comique (Stuart-Liff Collection)

Prévost and 'Manon Lescaut'

Vivienne Mylne

The Abbé Prévost was an extremely prolific writer. He produced not only three long novels, but some shorter novels, a variety of historical works, and a journal — *Pour et Contre* — along the lines of Addison's *Spectator*. He also translated a number of works from Latin and English, including Richardson's *Clarissa Harlowe*. These varied writings, which make up an impressive array of volumes, are nowadays largely neglected apart from a single short novel, *Manon Lescaut*.

It may seem surprising that an abbé should have created so vivid an account of passionate love, but Prévost was no ordinary cleric. Before taking his vows as a Benedictine in 1721, at the age of twenty-four, he had spent some time as a soldier. In 1728 he asked permission to transfer into a less strict branch of his Order. He left his monastery before the necessary formalities had been completed, and as this step led to the issuing of a warrant for his arrest, he then became a refugee. The next six years were spent in England and Holland, but he returned to Paris in 1734, managed to get his position regularised, and found a patron in the Prince de Conti. Even now his travels and trials were not over: he had to leave France in 1741 because he had helped the author of a clandestine journal, and spent about a year in Belgium and Germany before obtaining permission to return. From 1742 until his death in 1763 he led, at last, the settled life of a man of letters.

While he was in Holland, Prévost had fallen under the spell of a woman called Lecki Eckhardt. She was no innocent, having already had a long liaison with a Swiss colonel and borne him several children. Prévost got into difficulties through trying to satisfy her demands for money, and not only fled from the Hague leaving numerous debts behind him, but was even imprisoned, briefly, in London for forging a money order.

From the early nineteenth century onwards, it was generally assumed that this love-affair with Lecki was the source of *Manon Lescaut*: Prévost knew what it was to be overwhelmed by passion, even to the point of committing crimes for his beloved, and this knowledge accounted for the vividness of his portrayal of Des Grieux's love for Manon. Unfortunately — at least for those who find literary works more interesting if they reflect the author's real-life sufferings — this particular explanation is untenable. Research has proved that by the time he first met Lecki, Prévost must already have completed *Manon Lescaut*. The legend of Lecki as the inspiration for Manon still persists, but it *is* only a legend. Perhaps, in writing this story, Prévost was evoking memories of some earlier love-affair; there is no evidence, however, to support such a notion. The most we can deduce from the Lecki liaison is that Prévost proved himself to be the kind of man who, like Des Grieux, can be carried away by love.

On the face of it, *Manon Lescaut* does not seem very promising material for the stage, since the plot is somewhat repetitive. Three times over, when Manon and Des Grieux are living together, she leaves him for a wealthier 'protector'. Prévost manages to vary the attendant circumstances, and Des Grieux's reactions, in each case; but these are the kinds of fine detail which often have to be sacrificed when a novel is adapted for the theatre or the

Tito Schipa as Des Grieux in 1927 (Stuart-Liff Collection)

cinema. Any would-be adaptor might well feel that the basic plot of Prévost's work is lacking in variety.

The very way in which the story is presented might also appear to offer an obstacle to adaptation. After a few introductory pages, Des Grieux becomes the narrator, telling us his own story in the first person. Thus we see all the events solely from his point of view; he can excuse his own conduct, and present it in a way which is calculated to win our sympathy. As readers, we are never quite sure what Manon may be thinking or feeling, since it is Des Grieux's comments on her motives that build up our impression of her personality. She remains in fact a somewhat shadowy figure, a focus for Des Grieux's passion, but a character who rarely speaks and who cannot fully analyse or explain her own propensities.

Paradoxically, this very vagueness about Manon's inner life has contributed to her success: she has become, in the eyes of many readers, the enigmatic epitome of the eternal feminine, Woman the Enchantress at her most mysterious. Alfred de Musset, for instance, apostrophizes her as:

Manon! sphinx étonnant! véritable sirène!
Cœur trois fois féminin, Cléopâtre en paniers!

Her power to charm men is undeniable, for if Prévost tells us little about her feelings, we are left in no doubt concerning the effect she produces on others. It is noticeable that the people who are hostile towards her, such as Des Grieux's father, are men who have not met her. The rule which operates in general is: 'To see her is to love her' — or at any rate to desire her. With this

Lucrezia Bori as Manon, one of the leading interpreters of the role at the Met. (Stuart-Liff Collection)

capacity for ineluctably attracting men, she becomes a kind of counterpart to Don Juan. Just as he perpetually seeks to possess the women who cross his path, so every man who meets Manon seems to want her for his own. And just as Don Juan, after his inception in seventeenth-century Spain, rapidly became a European myth-figure, so Manon in her turn came to embody all that is bewitchingly attractive to every susceptible male.

In this respect she is part of a broader complex of ideas, which seems to have fascinated many eighteenth-century writers: the twin themes of seduction and the Fallen Woman. Richardson explored the field in *Pamela* and *Clarissa*; Crébillon *fils* and Fielding presented a more satirical view; Rousseau's Julie triumphantly regained her virtue after the fall; and in *Les Liaisons dangereuses* we see seduction taken to its cynical limits, together with extremes of pathos in the female victims. Manon, who preceded all these works, is unique: not only is she that rare phenomenon, the female seducer, but she manages to beguile men and lead them astray without conscious effort or intention on her part. Moreover, even if society punishes her as a fallen woman or a disruptive force, she retains her power of attraction. (In more recent times, both Nana and Lulu can be envisaged as variations on this theme.)

If any evidence is needed of Manon's status as a myth-figure, one has only to consider the scope and variety of the adaptations which she has inspired. The process begins in the eighteenth century with an anonymous play, which closed happily with the young couple's marriage. The nineteenth century produced two ballets (one of them Italian), three plays with or without interspersed songs, and an *opéra comique* by Scribe and Auger as well as the

Valerie Masterson as Manon and John Brecknock as Des Grieux in Act Two of the 1979 production by John Copley for ENO (photo: Donald Southern)

better known operas of Massenet and Puccini. Four more plays about Manon have been staged in the twentieth century; and the cinema, which treated the subject as early as 1908, has also provided four adaptations — including one with John Barrymore as Des Grieux. As this summary suggests, Manon has become a *persona* whose name evokes, even for people who have not read the novel, a character with specific attributes and qualities.

Prévost himself could hardly have foreseen how the public would react to his story of young love. It is indeed quite likely that he envisaged Des Grieux as a more interesting character than Manon; the full title which he gave to the work is, after all, *Histoire du chevalier Des Grieux et de Manon Lescaut*. And although we may nowadays call it a 'novel', the story as originally published was no more than a tail-piece, a slim seventh volume appended to a six-volume fictional autobiography, the *Mémoires et aventures d'un Homme de Qualité*. The first four volumes of this work had been favourably received. It is reasonable to suppose that Prévost, having written the story of Des Grieux's doomed love-affair, thought it would be better to attach it to the successful set of memoirs than to launch this little work on its own. Hence the introductory pages, where the Man of Quality sees Manon as a prisoner, on her way to Le Havre for deportation, and explains how Des Grieux later told him the whole story of his unhappy love. Nowadays some elements of that introduction may seem puzzling, since not one reader in a thousand has worked his way through the six-volume life of the Man of Quality or knows who he is supposed to be. But from the moment that Des Grieux starts his narrative, we can forget these distractions and concentrate on the Chevalier's story.

The public reaction to this seventh volume of the *Mémoires* was lively, and some publishers were quick to realize that the story could stand, and sell, on its own. The first separate edition was brought out in 1733, only two years after the work's initial appearance. From then on it was frequently reprinted, and as early as 1746 one edition carried the title *Histoire de Manon*, thus recognizing that she was the main attraction of the book.

Most of the early critics were prepared to admit that Prévost had created a work which could grip his readers' attention and win their sympathy, but this verdict was often accompanied by condemnation on moral grounds. Montesquieu, for instance, agreed that the poignant love-interest was bound to please the public, but stated bluntly that Des Grieux was a rogue and Manon a whore. (Prévost had tried to forestall such blame by inserting a preface which claimed that this was a cautionary tale, illustrating how a young man should *not* behave.) Criticisms of this kind, calling Manon a woman who 'brings dishonour on her sex', lead us on to the other crucial element of her behaviour: her infidelities.

Des Grieux is at pains to point out that Manon never betrayed him simply for money: all she wanted was a life of pleasure; what she could not face was boredom and a staid home-bound existence. She is the ultimate 'good-time girl'. This need for pleasure is strong enough to over-ride her attachment to Des Grieux, for she does love him — in her fashion.

Prévost seems to have felt that this point needed underlining, for some twenty years after the book's publication, he inserted a new episode in which, for once, Manon does *not* succumb to temptation. She repulses a rich Italian prince, and tells him to his face that he cannot compare with her handsome young lover. At this stage of events, however, Des Grieux is making enough money, by card-playing, for her to lead the kind of life she enjoys, so there is no real tug-of-war between her love and her desire for pleasure, and no real merit in her constancy. But any abstract discussion of moral values such as constancy or fidelity is inappropriate for Prévost's Manon: she is young — only fifteen or sixteen when the story begins — and a creature of impulse, hardly capable of reflecting on principles. She is therefore amoral rather than immoral. Only in the last stages of the book, during the Atlantic crossing and the couple's struggle for existence in Louisiana, does she begin to mature and develop a sense of responsibility. However, the repentant Manon, who might have made a good wife and mother, is not in accord with the myth. (One might as easily imagine Don Juan turning into a dutiful husband and a good father.) The image which persists is that of the charming but flighty girl who can always be tempted away from Des Grieux if life with him threatens to become dull.

Although Manon has stolen the limelight and come to typify faithless femininity, Des Grieux too can be seen as a type: he is the unfortunate man whose heart is captured by a woman who is unworthy of him. Nowadays it is Manon's infidelity which demonstrates her unworthiness, but Prévost's early readers would have seen her social status as another factor militating against Des Grieux's love — let alone his hopes of marrying her. After all, he belongs to the aristocracy, and marriage to a lower-class girl like Manon would be unthinkable. (Prévost stressed this gulf in his revised version of 1753: instead of coming, as previously, from a respectable family, Manon is here reduced to being 'of common birth'.) Her very name, a diminutive which is equivalent to 'Molly' or 'Moll', points up her plebeian origins.

Act Four at Covent Garden in 1955: Adele Leigh as Manon, John Lanigan as Des Grieux and Geraint Evans as Lescaut (Royal Opera House Archives)

Alan Opie as Lescaut in the gaming hall of the Hotel Transylvania at ENO (photo: John Garner)

Moreover when Des Grieux first meets Manon, he is only seventeen, and is portrayed as a young intellectual who has hitherto taken no interest in women. He is about to join the Order of the Knights of Malta (which is why he carries the title of 'Chevalier'), and members of this Order were not allowed to marry. After the first separation from Manon, he decides to enter the Church, so that the resumption of his liaison is all the more shocking. His friend Tiberge, himself a priest, acts throughout the novel as the representative of religion and virtue, and argues forcefully against this profane love. But for Des Grieux, his passion is so powerful that it justifies, or at least excuses, not merely his renunciation of the ecclesiastical life but also some actions which are clearly criminal: he takes to card-sharping and even kills a man in the course of his escape from detention. His love is therefore portrayed as degrading in every respect, since it runs counter to all the proper standards of a Christian and a gentleman of honour. Once it has passed through the filter of nineteenth-century Romanticism, however, the story acquires a different tone. This conflict, in which love is set against social and religious values, becomes a struggle which is interesting and even admirable, rather than degrading. Similarly, the stock figure of the 'prostitute with a heart of gold', as popularised in Dumas *fils's La Dame aux Camélias*, contributes to making Manon more glamorous and turns Des Grieux's blind love for her into a pathetic rather than a shameful passion.

There are two further aspects of Prévost's novel which do not accord with nineteenth-century attitudes. One is the hero's extreme sensibility: he repeatedly sheds floods of tears, and is proud of the intensity of feeling which shows him to be a finer and more sensitive soul than the common run of men. In the adaptations of the story, this trait is transmuted into a generalised Romantic capacity for elevated emotions. Secondly, Prévost's text is extremely restrained and euphemistic in its references to sexual love. (The couple's first love-making is glossed over with the remark: 'We defrauded the Church of its rights'.) Any stage performance, with the characters visible in the flesh before our eyes, is bound to illustrate more openly the erotic aspects of the story, which Prévost merely alludes to in the discreetest terms.

Jess Walters as the Count and John Lanigan as Des Grieux in Act Three at Covent Garden in 1955 (Royal Opera House Archives)

The gaming hall at the Hotel Transylvania in the ENO production, designed by Henry Bardon with costumes by Alix Stone (photo: Donald Southern)

Virginia McWatters as Manon and Heddle Nash as Des Grieux at Covent Garden in 1947 (Royal Opera House Archives)

Frances Alda as Manon at the Met. in 1905 (Stuart-Liff Collection)

In another respect, however, Prévost seems more modern: without going in for systematic 'realism' in the manner of Balzac or Dickens, he does provide a good many details which evoke Parisian life of the time, including for instance the gambling hells, the reformatory for prostitutes, and the dissolute soldiery personified by Lescaut. In particular, Parisians could have seen, in 1719 and 1720, the departure of several large contingents of prisoners, male and female, bound for Louisiana to help populate the colony. The deportation episode in the novel, where Manon reaches the depths of misery and misfortune, is turned by Massenet's librettists into the tragic climax leading to her death. (In Puccini's opera Manon dies, as in the novel, during the couple's flight from New Orleans.)

Only a pedant or a purist would, I think, complain about the way in which various adaptors have altered Prévost's story. He created a situation, and more particularly a heroine, with the power to crystallize a myth: the woman who is forever winning but can never be won, who promises fidelity but can always be lured away by the attractions of a life of pleasure. With the complementary character of the fixed and constant lover, prepared for any sacrifice if only he can share her life, this configuration has become public property, as free a source for new works as Oedipus, Faust or Don Juan. Because it can still speak to later generations, Prévost's little novel invites re-interpretation, and this is the penalty — or the reward — of its success.

Thematic Guide

Many of the themes from this opera have been identified in the articles by numbers in square brackets, which refer to the themes set out on these pages. The themes are also identified by the numbers in square brackets at the corresponding points in the libretto, so that the words can be related to the musical themes.

[9]
Andante cantabile/*bien chanté, expressif*

[10]
Andantino/*très calme*

p   *et léger*

[11]
MANON

Più mosso /*espressivo*

Ah! che-va - lier, je meurs d'ef - froi!   je meurs d'ef - froi!
Ah! che-va - lier, I'm so a - fraid!   I'm so a - fraid!

[12]
All° appassionato

[13]
Andante espressivo

[14]
MANON
Andante *sans lenteur*

espressivo

A - dieu, no-tre pe - ti - te ta - ble, Qui nous ré - u - nit si sou - vent!
Fare-well, our hap-py lit-tle ta - ble, This is where we sat ev-'ry day!

[15]
DES GRIEUX
Andante/*très calme*

En fer-mant les yeux je vois Là - bas_____
When I close my eyes I see so clear_____

[16]
All° moderato

[17]
LESCAUT
All° moderato

A quoi bon l'é - co-no-mie Quand on a trois dés en main!
Where's the fun in living cheaply When your dice is in your hand?

[18]
All^tto brillante

40

[19]

Andante tranquillo

[20]

COUNT

Andante/*simple et sans lenteur*

E - pou-se quel-que bra - ve fil - le,
Bring home to me a lov-ing daugh-ter,

[21]

DES GRIEUX

Sostenuto cantabile/*très calme*

Ah! fu-yez, douce i-mage à mon â - me trop chè-re;
Ah! Be gone dream of love, dream I lived for and cher-ished!

[22]

MANON

Andante/*with great charm, very affectionately*

N'est-ce plus ma main que ce-tte main pres - se? N'est-ce plus ma voix?
Don't you feel my hand here on your hand press-ing? Won't you turn and see?

[23]

Allegro moderato/*mystérieux et soutenu*

[24]

DES GRIEUX

Andante/*with passionate impetuosity*

Ma-non, sphinx é - ton-nant! Vé-ri - ta - ble si-rè — ne!
Ma-non, sphinx I a-dore; you have charmed me for e — ver!

[25]

Allegro moderato

[26]
Andante espressivo

[27]
MANON
Plus lent

Ah!	je	sens	u – ne pu	–	re flam – me
Ah!	I	feel	a	glo –	rious light

Dino Borgioli, a famous Des Grieux between the wars who sang regularly at Covent Garden and became vocal director of the New London Opera Company in 1949 (Stuart-Liff Collection)

42

Manon

Opéra Comique in Five Acts and Six Scenes
by J. Massenet

Text by Henri Meilhac and Philippe Gille,
based on the novel
Histoire du Chevalier des Grieux et de Manon Lescaut
by Antoine-François Prévost D'Exiles

English version by Edmund Tracey

Manon was first performed at the Opéra Comique, Paris on January 19, 1884. The first performance in England was in Liverpool on January 17, 1885. The first performance in the United States was at the Academy of Music, New York on December 23, 1885.

CHARACTERS

The Chevalier Des Grieux	*tenor*
The Count Des Grieux *his father*	*bass*
Lescaut *Manon's cousin*	*baritone*
Guillot de Morfontaine *a nobleman*	*tenor*
De Brétigny *a tax-collector*	*baritone*
Innkeeper	*baritone*
Two Guardsmen	*tenor, bass*
Porter of the Seminary	
Sergeant	*tenor*
Manon Lescaut	*soprano*
Poussette ⎤	*soprano*
Javotte ⎬ *actresses*	*mezzo-soprano*
Rosette ⎦	*mezzo-soprano*
Maid	*mezzo-soprano*

Men and Women of Amiens, Travellers, Post-boys and Porters, Men and Women of Paris, Gamblers, Guards.

Act One

The scene is the courtyard of an inn at Amiens. At the back there is a large gateway for carriages giving on to the street. To the right, downstage, is a pavilion which may be reached by several steps. To the left, an arbour in front of which is a well and a stone bench. Upstage, behind the arbour and a little further forward, is the entrance to the inn.

Scene One. *Brétigny, Guillot de Morfontaine, Poussette, Javotte, Rosette. As the curtain rises we can see Brétigny at the pavilion door. Guillot, his kerchief in his hand, is below on the bottom step.*

GUILLOT
(*calling*)

Hola! Hey! Is there no-one there?	Holà! hé! monsieur l'hôtelier,
Or must we shout until we're hoarse,	Combien de temps faut-il crier,
Before you condescend to hear us?	Avant que vous daigniez entendre?

BRETIGNY

Some more to drink!	Nous avons soif!

GUILLOT

Something to eat!	Nous avons faim!

BRETIGNY

How does he dare to keep us waiting?	Vous moquez-vous de faire attendre?

BRETIGNY, GUILLOT

My God! Will he never appear?	Morbleu! viendrez-vous à la fin?

GUILLOT

I am Guillot-Morfontaine!	Foi de Guillot-Morfontaine
Is he mad to keep us here,	C'est par trop de cruauté
Wealthy noblemen like us?	Pour des gens de qualité!

BRETIGNY
(*angrily*)

If he's dead, wouldn't that explain it?	Il est mort, la chose est certaine!

GUILLOT
(*angrily*)

Can't he hear? Can't he hear?	Il est mort! Il est mort!

POUSSETTE
(*at the window, laughing*)

No need to be in such a rage!	Allons, messieurs, point de courroux!

GUILLOT, BRETIGNY

Will no-one serve us? He doesn't hear!	Que faut-il faire? Il n'entend pas!

JAVOTTE, POUSSETTE, ROSETTE

Then we must call him, and keep on calling!	On le rappelle! On le harcelle!

JAVOTTE, POUSSETTE, ROSETTE, BRETIGNY, GUILLOT

Come on, wake up, you inside!	Voyons, monsieur l'hôtelier!
Show your hospitality!	Montrez-vous hospitalier!
Do not let us die of hunger!	Sauvez-nous de la famine,
If you don't we'll have to hang you!	Sinon l'on vous extermine!
Show your hospitality!	Soyez donc hospitalier!
Come on, wake up, you inside!	Voyons, monsieur l'hôtelier!

BRETIGNY
(*listening*)

And so . . . What now? . . . He doesn't answer.	Eh bien! . . . Eh quoi! . . . pas de réponse!

He doesn't answer!   Pas de réponse?

BRETIGNY

He ignores all our remonstrations!   Il est sourd à notre semonce!

POUSSETTE, JAVOTTE, ROSETTE

Let's start again!   Recommençons!

GUILLOT

Not too much noise,   Pas trop de bruit!
For that affects my appetite!   Cela redouble l'appétit.

ALL TOGETHER

Come on, wake up, you inside!   Voyons, monsieur l'hôtelier!

Scene Two. *The same. The innkeeper appears in his doorway.*

BRETIGNY
(*in a burst of joy and surprise*)

Ah, at last, here's the scoundrel!   Ah! voilà, le coupable!

GUILLOT
(*so angry that he is ludicrous*)

Are you trying to starve us?   Réponds-nous, misérable!

INNKEEPER
(*indignant*)

I never let you down!   Moi, vous abandonner!
I've only this to say: Let dinner now be   Je ne dirai qu'un mot: qu'on serve le dîner!
served!

Enter, from the inn, waiters carrying plates. The waiters proceed slowly and rather solemnly towards the summer house. [1]

INNKEEPER
(*importantly*)

Hors d'œuvres to start . . .   Hors d'œuvres de choix . . .

ALL

Good!   Bien!

INNKEEPER

. . . all with delicate spices . . .   . . . et diverses épices . . .
Some fish . . . or fowl!   Poisson, poulet . . .

ALL

Superb!   Parfait!

JAVOTTE

I want fish!   Du poisson!

GUILLOT

I want fowl!   Du poulet!

BRETIGNY

Superb!   Parfait!

POUSSETTE

O sweetest dispensation!   O douce providence!

ALL

See, they're in formation!   Voilà qu'en cadence
Ready to begin!   On vient nous servir!

INNKEEPER

You see! Ready to begin!   Voyez! on vient vous servir!

(*urging persistently*)

Here are exquisite shellfish!   Un buisson d'écrevisses!

POUSSETTE, JAVOTTE, ROSETTE, GUILLOT

Exquisite shellfish!   Des écrevisses!

INNKEEPER

Let me recommend this old wine . . .   Et pour arroser le repas,
With your food!   De vieux vins . . .

GUILLOT
(*to the waiters*)

Do not shake the wine!   Ne les troublez pas!

INNKEEPER

To complete the list of the courses: Et pour compléter les services,
Here's a special pâté!   Le pâté de canard!

ALL

A pâté!   Un pâté!

INNKEEPER
(*puffing himself up*)

Much more than that: a work of art!   Non pas, messieurs! un objet d'art!

GUILLOT

It's true!   Vraiment!

BRETIGNY

Superb!   Parfait!

BRETIGNY, GUILLOT, THE LADIES

O sweetest dispensation!   O douce providence
Blessed invitation,   Voilà qu'en cadence,
Ready to begin!   On vient nous servir!
What a consolation,   O sort délectable,
When you want to eat,   Lorsque l'on a faim,
Seeing such a treat.   De se mettre enfin,
All ready! Ready to begin!   A table! On vient nous servir!
  We're ready!   A table!

INNKEEPER

You see!   Voyez!
Ready to begin!   On vient vous servir!
All this preparation,   Il est préférable
When you want to eat,   Et même très sain,
Makes it such a treat.   D'attendre la faim.
Now we're in formation!   Mettez-vous à table!
Ready to begin.   On vient vous servir!
You're ready! We're ready!   A table! A table!

All go into the summer house, the door and window of which close again.

Scene Three. *The innkeeper remains on stage alone.*

INNKEEPER
(*speaking*)

It's very nice to sit down to dinner! . . .   C'est très bien de dîner! . . . Il faut aussi
  Paying the bill isn't so popular!   payer!
I'd better make sure . . . Lord bless me,   Et je vais . . . Mais, au fait, pensons au
  what am I doing! I'd nearly forgotten   chevalier
  Chevalier des Grieux. It's getting late . . .   Des Grieux! . . . Le temps passe,
And I promised to keep a seat for him   Et j'ai promis de retenir sa place
  in this evening's coach.   Au premier coche . . .
     (*He turns to go upstairs and sees the townspeople about to invade the inn.*)
Ah, here they come,   Eh, mais, voilà,

The good	Déjà
people of Amiens,	La ribambelle
In all their finery . . . Looking to see	Des bons bourgeois! . . . Ils viennent regarder
If there's a pretty girl	Si l'on peut lorgner
They can flirt with,	Quelque belle,
Or some poor traveller to make fun of! [2]	Ou se moquer de quelque voyageur! . . .

(*singing, sententiously*)

The people here all like to know what's going on!	J'ai remarqué que l'homme est très observateur!

(*He goes into his office.*)

Scene Four. *Men and women of Amiens, then Lescaut and two guards, travellers, post boys and porters; then Manon. The inn clock strikes. The townspeople gradually pour into the inn.*

TOWNSPEOPLE
(*calmly*)

Listen, the bell is ringing.	Entendez-vous la cloche,
Now the coach is arriving.	Voici l'heure du coche!
We must see this!	Il faut tout voir!
Some on their own, some with a lady.	Les voyageurs, les voyageuses
We'll see them all!	Il faut tout voir!
We miss nothing at all!	Pour nous c'est un devoir!

(*Lescaut enters, followed by two guardsmen.*)

LESCAUT
(*addressing the gentlemen*)

But are you sure this is the right place?	C'est bien ici l'hôtellerie
Is the coach from Arras due to stop here tonight?	Où le coche d'Arras va tantôt s'arrêter?

GUARDS

This is the place!	[3] C'est bien ici!

LESCAUT
(*dismissing them*)

Goodnight!	Bonsoir!

GUARDS
(*crying out*)

Really you can't be serious	Quelle plaisanterie!
Lescaut. Won't you come for a drink?	Lescaut, tu pourrais nous quitter?

LESCAUT
(*good humouredly*)

I will! So why don't you wait in the tavern	Jamais! Allez à l'auberge voisine;
Where they sell a delicious wine:	On y vend un clairet joyeux;
My little cousin won't be long.	Je vais attendre ma cousine,
Then I will be ready to dine.	Et je vous rejoins tous les deux!

GUARDS

You won't forget?	Rappelle-toi?

LESCAUT
(*offended*)

What did you say? 'You won't forget?'	Vous m'insultez, c'est imprudent.

GUARDS
(*begging*)

Lescaut!	Lescaut!

LESCAUT
(*pleased and insolent*)

That's right. While I'm capable of thinking	C'est bon! Je perdrais la mémoire,
I'll never tire of drinking!	Quand il s'agit de boire!

(with an air of authority, cunningly changing his tone)

So why not wait there in the tavern	Allez! à l'auberge voisine
Where they sell a delicious wine!	On y vend un clairet joyeux!
My little cousin won't be long —	Je vais attendre ma cousine!
So off with you, fill up your glass!	Allez trinquer en m'attendant!
Off with you both, I'll join you soon!	En m'attendant, allez trinquer!

Exeunt two guards by the door at the back. The bell is heard once more and the street fills with postboys, porters carrying trunks, boxes and suitcases, and travellers of both sexes scurrying about for their luggage.

TOWNSPEOPLE
(merrily)

Here they are!   Les voilà!

The coach is seen arriving upstage and the travellers get out.

AN OLD LADY
(tidying up)

My hair's untidy! My gown is crumpled!   Oh! ma coiffure!... oh! ma toilette!

TOWNSPEOPLE
(laughing)

Oh, she is looking rather rumpled!   Voyez-vous pas cette coquette!

A TRAVELLER (male)

Hey, porter, here!   Hé! le porteur!

PORTER
(in a bad humour)

One moment please!   Dans un instant!

TOWNSPEOPLE
(laughing)

Ah, what a silly looking fellow!   Ah! le singulier personnage!

A TRAVELLER (female)

I can't find my cage and my parrot.   Où sont mes oiseaux et ma cage?

FOUR TRAVELLERS
(calling)

Hey! Come and help!   Hé, postillon!

A TRAVELLER

Where's my trunk?   Ma malle!

A TRAVELLER

My basket!   Mon panier!

POSTBOYS AND PORTERS
(disengaging themselves)

In a moment!   Dans un moment!

TRAVELLERS
(shouting with all their might)

Now will you give us all our luggage!   Donnez à chacun son bagage!

POSTBOYS

Let's have less racket!   Moins de tapage!

TRAVELLERS

Come on! Come on! Come on!	Voyons! voyons! voyons!
God! What a fuss and what a bore	Dieux! quel tracas et quel tourment
When people have to go by carriage!	Quand il faut monter en voiture!
Ah! I declare you would be well advised	Ah! je le jure on ferait bien,
To make a will before.	De faire avant son testament.

49

POSTBOYS, PORTERS AND TOWNSPEOPLE

No! No! No!
Ah! Always groans and shouts galore!
They're always groaning in a carriage!
Oh! When they have to board a carriage
Or they have to disembark!

Non! non! non!
Ah! c'est à se damner vraiment,
Chacun d'eux gémit et murmure
Rien qu'en montant dans la voiture,
Et recommence en descendant!

TRAVELLERS
(running after the postboys)

I swear I am the first!

Je suis { le premier!
la première!

POSTBOYS AND PORTERS
(and the townspeople mimicking them)

You're the last! No!

Le dernier! Non!

Manon, who has just come out of the crowd, looks on all this hubbub with astonishment. [4]

LESCAUT
(observing her in turn)

Now I am certain
This charming creature here is Manon, my
  dear cousin!

Eh! j'imagine
Que cette belle enfant, c'est Manon! . . . ma
  cousine!

(to Manon, frankly)

I am Lescaut.

Je suis Lescaut.

MANON
(slightly surprised)

Ah, is it you . . .

Vous, mon cousin?

(simply and without restraint)

Give me a kiss!

Embrassez-moi!

LESCAUT

Ah, with all my heart I'll oblige.
My word but she's a lovely creature!
She really does the family credit!

Mais très volontiers, sur ma foi! . . .
Morbleu! c'est une belle fille
Qui fait honneur à la famille!

MANON
(with embarrassment)

Ah cousin please, do not be cross!

Ah! mon cousin, excusez-moi!

LESCAUT
(aside)

She's really charming!

Elle est charmante!

MANON
(with charm and emotion)

I'm so confused, my poor head's reeling, [4]
I can't describe just what I'm feeling!
Cousin be kind! Please don't be cross.
I find myself quite at a loss . . .
I think my head, my poor head's reeling!

Je suis encore tout étourdie,
Je suis encore tout engourdie!
Ah mon cousin, excusez-moi;
Excusez un moment d'émoi,
Je suis encore tout étourdie!

(with animation)

Ah, please forgive my silly chatter.
I found the journey so exciting!

Pardonnez à mon bavardage,
J'en suis à mon premier voyage!

(in narrative fashion)

The moment the coach had started
I looked around, my eyes were wide,
Every village and wood and meadow . . .
The people too, on every side . . .

Le coche s'éloignait à peine,
Que j'admirais de tous mes yeux,
Les hameaux, les grands bois, la plaine,
Les voyageurs jeunes et vieux!

(changing her tone)

Ah, cousin, don't be cross with me!
I found it so exciting!

Ah! mon cousin, excusez-moi!
C'est mon premier voyage!

(continuing her narrative)

Watching it fly by was so lovely . . .
The trees all waving in the wind!

Je regardais fuir, curieuse,
Les arbres frissonnant au vent!

I felt so free, so free and happy,	Et j'oubliais, toute joyeuse,
I quite forgot what lay in store:	Que je partais pour le couvent!
The convent door!	Pour le couvent!
I found it so wildly exciting . . .	Devant tant de choses nouvelles,
Now do not laugh, but I declare	Ne riez pas si je vous dis
I really felt that I was flying,	Que je croyais avoir des ailes,
Yes, flying up to Paradise!	Et m'envoler au paradis!
Ah, cousin dear!	Oui, mon cousin,
Then there came a moment of sadness!	Puis, j'eus un moment de tristesse . . .
And I wept . . . I can't tell you why!	Je pleurais . . . je ne sais pas quoi?

(changing her tone)

A minute later I was laughing with	L'instant d'après, je le confesse,
delight . . .	

(bursting out into peals of laughter)

Ah! how I laughed, but I can't tell you why!	Je riais sans savoir pourquoi!

(embarrassed)

Ah! Cousin, please . . . I've never been	Ah, mon cousin, excusez-moi! Ah! mon
away from home before!	cousin, pardon!
I'm so confused my poor head's reeling! [4]	Je suis encore tout étourdie,
I can't describe just what I'm feeling.	Je suis encore tout engourdie!

(delivered in a lively manner)

Ah, please forgive my silly chatter.	Pardonnez à mon bavardage,
I found the journey so exciting!	Je suis à mon premier voyage!

Much activity on stage. The travellers, preceded by the postboys, pour into the courtyard. A bell rings for the departure of the coach. Reprise of the chorus. The stage gradually empties. The crowd goes off, leaving Lescaut and Manon alone.

LESCAUT
(speaking)

Wait here, there's a good girl!	Attendez-moi, soyez bien sage.
I'll go and find your things.	Je vais chercher votre bagage!

Exit Lescaut.

Scene Five. *Guillot appears on the balcony of the summer house.*

GUILLOT
(speaking)

You miserable innkeeper! Are we never	Hôtelier de malheur! il est donc entendu
To have more wine?	Que nous n'aurons jamais de vin!

(seeing Manon)

Ah, what a beauty!	Ciel! qu'ai-je vu?

(descending)

Mademoiselle! . . . hem! hem! . . .	Mademoiselle! . . . hem! hem! . . .
Mademoiselle.	Mademoiselle . . .

(aside)

I've never been so dazzled	Ce qui se passe en ma cervelle
In my whole life!	Est inouï!

MANON
(aside, laughing)

What a funny looking man!	Cet homme est fort drôle, ma foi!

GUILLOT

Mademoiselle, listen to me!	Mademoiselle, écoutez-moi!
My name is Guillot, Guillot de Morfontaine.	On me nomme Guillot, Guillot de Morfontaine;
I have a purse full of gold,	De louis d'or ma caisse est pleine,
But I'd give it all away	Et j'en donnerais beaucoup pour
Just for one tender word from you . . .	Obtenir de vous un seul mot d'amour . . .
There now, what do you say?	J'ai fini, qu'avez-vous à dire? . . .

I think I ought to be very angry with you . . . but all I want to do is laugh . . .

Que je me fâcherais si je n'aimais mieux rire . . .

Manon bursts out laughing, as do also Brétigny, Javotte, Poussette and Rosette, who have just come out on the balcony.

BRETIGNY

My good Guillot, what on earth are you doing?
Why do you keep us waiting?

Eh bien, Guillot, que faites-vous?
Nous vous attendons!

GUILLOT

Go to hell!

Au diable les fous!

POUSSETTE

You ought to be ashamed of yourself, at your age!

N'avez-vous pas honte? . . . à votre âge! . . .

JAVOTTE, AND ROSETTE

At his age!!

A votre âge!!

BRETIGNY

Wait a moment! This time our foolish friend
Has stumbled on a real treasure. I never
saw such a sweet expression
On so charming a face.

Cette fois-ci, le drôle a par hasard
Découvert un trésor. Jamais plus doux
regard
N'illumina plus gracieux visage . . .

POUSSETTE, JAVOTTE AND ROSETTE
(singing and laughing at Guillot)

Come away, Guillot, come away!   [5]
This infatuation beware!
Dearest friend Guillot, you must take care!
Come away or one day you will have to pay.
Now come away, Guillot, come away,
Or one day you will have to pay!

Revenez, Guillot, revenez!
Dieu sait où vous mène un faux pas?
Cher ami, Guillot, n'en faites pas!
Revenez! Vous allez vous casser le nez!
Non! Revenez donc, Guillot! Revenez!
Vous allez vous casser le nez!

BRETIGNY
(speaking)

Come on Guillot, leave the girl alone!
Come back and finish your dinner!

Allons, Guillot, laissez mademoiselle,
Et revenez, l'on vous appelle! . . .

GUILLOT
(getting impatient)

Yes, yes, I'll be with you in a minute.

Oui, je reviens dans un moment.

BRETIGNY

Guillot, leave the girl alone . . .

Guillot, laissez mademoiselle! . . .

GUILLOT
(in a low voice to Manon)

Pretty child, listen to me.
In a little while my coachman will come into the courtyard.
When you see him it will mean
That my carriage is waiting. You can take it if you wish . . .
Afterwards . . . well . . . I think you understand!

Ma mignonne, un mot seulement!
De ma part, tout à l'heure, un postillon viendra . . .
Quand vous l'apercevrez, cela signifiera:
Qu'une voiture attend, que vous pouvez la prendre . . .
Et qu'après . . . vous devez comprendre . . .

Lescaut has just entered and places himself in front of Guillot as the latter turns to re-enter the pavilion.

LESCAUT
(brusquely to Guillot)

Now then Monsieur! . . .

Plaît-il, monsieur?

GUILLOT
(speechless, stammering)

Monsieur ...   Monsieur?

LESCAUT
Speak up!   Eh bien?

Don't be shy ...   Vous disiez?

GUILLOT

Don't know what you mean!   Je ne disais rien!

(retreating in spite of himself towards the summerhouse)

BRETIGNY AND THE LADIES

Come away Guillot, come away!   Revenez, Guillot, revenez,
This infatuation beware!   Dieu sait où nous mène un faux pas!

Laughing, they all go into the summerhouse.

Scene Six. *Lescaut, Manon, Guards.*

LESCAUT
(to Manon, seriously)

What did he say, Manon?   Il vous parlait, Manon?

MANON
(lightly and with animation)

It really wasn't my fault.   Ce n'était pas ma faute ...

LESCAUT

Never! I think too well of you my little cousin,   Certes! et j'ai de vous opinion trop haute
To be upset.   Pour me fâcher.

GUARDS
(to Lescaut)

Lescaut where have you been?   Eh bien, tu ne viens pas?
We cannot play at dice or at cards without   Les cartes et les dés nous attendent là-bas!
you!

[6]

LESCAUT

Agreed! This innocent young beauty   Je viens, mais à cette jeunesse
Needs a word of warning and wisdom: Permettez d'abord que j'adresse

(conceitedly)

And I have never neglected my duty.   Quelques conseils tout remplis de sagesse!...

GUARDS
(submissively, respectfully)

Yes, he must do his duty.   Ècoutons la sagesse.

LESCAUT
(self-importantly, to Manon)

Now then, look me straight in the eye! [6]   Regardez-moi bien dans les yeux!
I have received an invitation.   Je vais tout près à la caserne,
These young soldiers need my advice   Discuter avec ces messieurs
About a certain situation.   De certain point qui les concerne.
In a little while I'll be back ...   Attendez-moi donc un instant,
    I won't be long.   Un seul moment ...

Now don't you stir, do what I say,   Ne bronchez pas, soyez gentille,
And don't forget, my dear young girl,   Et n'oubliez pas, mon cher cœur,
I will always cherish the pearl   Que je suis gardien de l'honneur
    Of family honour!   De la famille!

If you should hear proposals made   [6]   Si par hasard, quelque imprudent
To run off with a stranger,   Vous tenait un propos frivole,
Do not worry or be afraid ...   Dans la crainte d'un accident,
For you might find yourself in danger!   Ne dites pas une parole!

53

Bid him wait and I won't be long . . .
  I'll soon be back!

Priez-le d'attendre un instant,
  Un seul moment . . .

Now don't you stir, do what I say,
And don't forget, my dear young girl,
I will always cherish the pearl
  Of family honour!

Ne bronchez pas, soyez gentille,
Et n'oubliez pas, mon cher cœur,
Que je suis gardien de l'honneur
  De la famille!

(to the Guardsmen signalling them to go)

And now my friends, we three will go and see
If the goddess of luck is making eyes at me.

Et maintenant, voyons à qui de nous
La déesse du jeu va faire les yeux doux!

(as he leaves, he turns back to Manon)

Now don't you stir. Do what I tell you!

Ne bronchez pas, soyez gentille!

Exit.

Scene Seven. *Manon.*

MANON
(simply)

I will stay here . . . I have no choice!
I must try not to think! I get lost in my day-
dreams,
In ideas which destroy all my peace of mind!

No dreams for me!

Restons ici, puisqu'il le faut!
Attendons . . . sans penser! . . . Evitons ces
folies,
Ces projets qui mettaient ma raison en
défaut!

Ne rêvons plus! . . .

[4]

Manon seems lost in thought. Her face shows her internal struggle. Then suddenly, simply, she turns her glance to the summerhouse, where Poussette, Javotte and Rosette are. She rises.

I think these women are so pretty!
And the necklace of pearl that the youngest
one wore! . . .
Ah! I love the way they all glitter!
And all their fashionable chatter.
I admire them all more and more!

Combien ces femmes sont jolies! . . .
La plus jeune portait un collier de grains
d'or! . . .
Ah! comme ces riches toilettes
Et ces parures si coquettes
Les rendaient plus belles encore! . . .

(sad and resigned) [7]

No use Manon, no use in dreaming.
Why do you forget what's in store?
Give up these longings and this scheming:
Leave them all at the convent door!

Voyons, Manon, plus de chimères,
Où va ton esprit en rêvant?
Laisse ces désirs éphémères
A la porte de ton couvent!

(changing her tone)

Yet even so, for a lady of leisure
How lovely always to be free!

Et cependant, pour mon âme ravie
En elles tout est séduisant!

(with a burst of desire)

Ah! how amusing it would be
To spend my life in endless pleasure!
Ah! No use Manon, no use in dreaming . . .
Why do you forget what's in store?

Ah! Combien ce doit être amusant
De s'amuser toute une vie! . . .
Ah! Voyons, Manon, plus de chimères . . .
Où va ton esprit en rêvant?

(half weeping, half smiling)

No use Manon! No use Manon!
You mustn't waste your time in dreaming!

Voyons, Manon! Voyons, Manon!
Plus de désirs, plus de chimères!

Scene Eight. *Manon, then Des Grieux.*

MANON
(catching sight of Des Grieux)

There's someone here! Quick! Back to my
stone seat!

Quelqu'un! Vite à mon banc de pierre!

She promptly sits down, assuming the posture Lescaut had shown her.

DES GRIEUX
(comes downstage without seeing Manon) [8]

Now that I'm ready to depart . . .

J'ai marqué l'heure du départ . . .

(dreamily)

All at once . . . I feel I must stay here!

J'hésitais . . . chose singulière! . . .

(resolutely)

Come on, just a day in the coach	Enfin, demain soir au plus tard
And then I'll see my father! Yes, I can see him smiling,	J'embrasserai mon père! . . . Oui, je le vois sourire,
He's the one I can always trust!	Et mon cœur ne me trompe pas!
There he is, calls my name . . . [8]	Je le vois, il m'appelle
I take him in my arms!	Et je lui tends les bras!

Unconsciously Des Grieux has turned towards Manon. He speaks ecstatically as if beholding a vision.

Oh heaven! . . . Am I dreaming? . . . Is she a delusion?	O ciel! . . . Est-ce un rêve? . . . Est-ce la folie?
My soul is in a turmoil. Just as though my whole life	D'où vient ce que j'éprouve? On dirait que ma vie
Came to an end . . . or a beginning! I feel as if I'm led	Va finir . . . ou commence! . . . Il semble qu'une main
Along a path by a hand hard as steel . . .	De fer me mène en un autre chemin
I have no choice . . . it draws me here beside her . . .	Et malgré moi m'entraîne devant elle! . . .

Little by little Des Grieux has drawn nearer to Manon, who has risen and smiles at him in amazement. [9]

DES GRIEUX
(speaking timidly)

Mademoiselle . . .	Mademoiselle . . .

MANON

Monsieur?	Eh quoi?

DES GRIEUX
(moved)

Forgive me . . .	Pardonnez-moi!
I don't know . . . It's an impulse . . . I'm no longer my own master . . .	Je ne sais . . . j'obéis . . . je ne sais plus mon maître . . .

(gradually more ardent)

I'm sure	Je vous vois
I've never seen you before,	J'en suis sûr, pour la première fois

(tender and restrained)

Yet in my heart I feel as if I'd always known you!	Et mon cœur cependant vient de vous reconnaître!
Will you tell me your name?	Et je sais votre nom . . .

MANON
(simply)

Yes, my name is Manon.	On m'appelle Manon . . .

DES GRIEUX
(with feeling)

Manon!	Manon!

MANON
(aside)

He looks so kind and sweet!	Que son regard est tendre!
And what pleasure it gives me to hear him!	Et que j'ai de plaisir à l'entendre! . . .

DES GRIEUX

All I said was quite mad . . . Forgive my foolish words!	Ces paroles d'un fou, veuillez les pardonner!

MANON
(simply)

Ah no, don't take them back . . .	Comment les condamner!
They went right to my heart. I was charmed by their music!	Elles charment le cœur en charmant les oreilles!
If I knew such sweet sounding phrases, I would say them for you!	J'en voudrais savoir de pareilles Pour vous les répéter!

DES GRIEUX
(enraptured)

You are a goddess!
A being apart!
Manon, I worship you as ruler
Of my heart.

Enchanteresse
Au charme vainqueur!
Manon! Vous êtes la maîtresse
De mon cœur!

MANON

Charming words! What feverish longing
Stirs my heart!

Mots charmants, enivrantes fièvres
Du bonheur!

DES GRIEUX

O Manon! Now you are the ruler
Of my heart!

O Manon! Vous êtes maîtresse
De mon cœur!

(after a long silence)

Now, dear Manon ...

Ah! parlez-moi!

MANON

I am poor and of humble parents.

Je ne suis qu'une pauvre fille ...

(smiling)

I'm really not a bad girl ... But at home
They abuse me because I'm lively
And I love having fun, so they're sending me
off to a convent.
Now you know the story of Manon ...
Of Manon Lescaut! ...

Je ne suis pas mauvaise ... Mais souvent
On m'accuse dans ma famille
D'aimer trop le plaisir! ... On me met au
couvent ... tout à l'heure ...
Et c'est là l'histoire de Manon,
De Manon Lescaut! ...

DES GRIEUX
(ardently)

No, I will not believe
That fate is so unkind,
That one so lovely and so young
Could be buried away in the gloom of a
convent.

Non, je ne veux pas croire
A cette cruauté!
Que tant de charmes et de beauté
Soient voués à jamais à la tombe vivante!

MANON

And yet, it's true! It is the will
Of God that I kneel as his servant.
Alas I know no way of escape ... I must go!

Mais c'est, hélas! ... la volonté
Du ciel dont je suis la servante,
Puisqu'un malheur si grand ne peut être
évité!

DES GRIEUX
(firmly)

No! I'll not let them rob you of your
precious freedom!

Non! Votre liberté ne sera pas ravie! ...

MANON
(joyously)

But how?

Comment?

DES GRIEUX

Now trust in me
As your friend: Chevalier Des Grieux.

Au chevalier
Des Grieux, vous pouvez vous fier!

MANON
(with spirit)

Ah, my life is yours, my very being!

Ah! Je vous devrai plus que la vie!

DES GRIEUX
(passionately)

Ah, Manon! I'll never let you go!
I'll search throughout the world, I will
discover
Some secret haven for me and my lover ...
And carry you there in my arms!

Ah! Manon! Vous ne partirez pas!
Dussé-je aller chercher au bout du monde
Une retraite inconnue et profonde
Et vous y porter dans mes bras!

MANON

I live for you and you only! For you!	A vous ma vie et mon âme! ... A vous!
My heart is yours for ever, evermore.	A vous toute ma vie, à jamais!

DES GRIEUX

You are a goddess Manon,	Enchanteresse! ... Manon,
I worship you as ruler of my heart.	Vous êtes la maitresse de mon cœur!

At this moment the postboy whom Guillot has told to follow Manon's orders appears upstage.
Manon looks at him, thinks a moment, then smiles.

MANON
(gaily)

Now as it happens	Par aventure,
I think we are in luck ...	Peut-être avons-nous mieux:
We have a carriage.	Une voiture!
It's ordered by a lord ... He was here	La chaise d'un seigneur ... il faisait les
making eyes	doux yeux
At Manon.	A Manon.

(slyly)

Take revenge.	Vengez-vous!

DES GRIEUX

Take revenge?	Mais comment?

MANON

	We'll escape	Tous les deux
In his coach!	Prenons-là! ...	

DES GRIEUX
(to the postboy who goes off at once)

Yes, to Paris.	Soit, partons!

MANON
(disturbed)

Ah wait ... leave together?	Eh quoi, partir ensemble? ...

DES GRIEUX
(enraptured)

Yes, Manon! You're mine now. Be my love.	Oui, Manon! Le ciel nous rassemble!

DES GRIEUX AND MANON
(with emotion and charm)

Live with me, be my love ... live with { me. / you.	Nous vivrons à Paris tous les deux,
Let our hearts beat as one ...	Et nos cœurs amoureux,
Bound together we will be!	L'un à l'autre, enchaînés
Yes, in Paris you'll see	Pour jamais réunis

(gaily)

How our hearts and minds agree!	N'y vivront que des jours bénis!
You are } free! / I am	À Paris!

DES GRIEUX
(approaching Manon tenderly; with deep feeling)

Then I'll give you my name in marriage!	Et mon nom deviendra le vôtre!

(He bends towards her to embrace her, then recovers himself. With feeling, half spoken:)

Ah, Manon!	Ah! Pardon! ...

MANON

In my eyes now surely you see	Dans mes yeux vous devez bien voir
You'd have no cause to feel regret ...	Que je ne puis vous en vouloir;

(almost spoken)

And yet I know it's wrong!	Et cependant, c'est mal! ...

Peals of laughter come from the summer-house.

MANON
(remembering)

Ah! There they are again!   Ce sont elles!

DES GRIEUX

What's the matter?   Qu'avez-vous? . . .

MANON
(in confusion)

Nothing! Those girls are so pretty!   Rien! . . . ces femmes si belles! . . .

LESCAUT
(offstage, tipsy)

You wait till tonight. I'll win it all back at   Ce soir, vous rendrez tout au cabaret voisin!
the tavern next door.

DES GRIEUX
(frightened)

Ah!   Là! . . .

MANON
(frightened)

That's my cousin coming back!   C'est la voix de mon cousin!

DES GRIEUX

Come away!   Viens! partons! . . .

Poussette, Javotte and Rosette are heard singing and laughing in the summer-house.

MANON
(pausing in indecision; aside, in a burst of desire)

Ah, how delightful it would be   Ah! Combien ce doit être amusant
(very pointedly)

To spend my life in fun and laughter!   De s'amuser toute une vie! . . .

BOTH

Ah! away!   Viens! partons!

They both flee.

Scene Nine. *Lescaut then Guillot; Townspeople, then Brétigny, Javotte, Poussette, Rosette and the Innkeeper.*

LESCAUT
(entering drunk)

What a game! I didn't win a trick.   Plus un sou! Le tour est très plaisant!
(calling; looking for her; stupefied)

Eh! Manon! Hey! Where's she gone to?   Hé! . . . Manon! . . . Quoi! Disparue!
Manon!   holà!

GUILLOT
(going down the steps softly; cautiously)

I wonder if she's here.   Je veux la retrouver! . . .

LESCAUT
(seeing him and barring the way)

Ah, it's you! High and mighty!   Ah! c'est vous! Le gros homme!

GUILLOT
(drawing back)

What?   Hein?

LESCAUT

What have you done with Manon? You, tell   Vous avez pris Manon, vous, rendez-la!
the truth.

58

GUILLOT
(*terrified*)

Not so loud!   Taisez-vous!

LESCAUT
(*shouting all the louder*)

I want her back!   Rendez-la-moi!

Gradually, at the sound of Lescaut's shouting, the townspeople and the innkeeper have come from all sides. Laughing, they point the two quarrelling men out to each other.

GUILLOT
(*to Lescaut, pointing at all the people*)

Now half the town   Regardez donc comme
Is woken up with all your shouting!   Vous attirez la foule!

LESCAUT

Ah, bah! What's that to me!   Ah! bah! ça m'est égal!
(*to the people*)
He's dishonoured our name!   Il a pris notre honneur! . . .
(*to Guillot*)
I swear I'll leave my mark   C'est un trop beau régal
On your repulsive face!   Pour ton vilain museau! . . .

GUILLOT
(*terrified*)

Oh what a nightmare!   Quelle aventure!

INNKEEPER AND CHORUS

Come on! What have you done?   Voyons, expliquez-vous!

GUILLOT

Wait! Gently, if you please;   Soit! . . . mais très doucement,
There is no need for all this shouting!   très doucement et sans injure!

LESCAUT
(*still more loudly*)

Now speak out . . . and nothing but the   Répondez catégoriquement;
   truth:
Where is Manon?   Je veux Manon!

INNKEEPER

Who? Is it the young lady?   Quoi! cette jeune fille?
She left for Paris. A gentleman took her! . . . Elle est partie avec un jeune homme! . . .
   Do you hear?   Écoutez!

In the distance the sound of a carriage is heard.

GUILLOT
(*in despair*)

Oh God!   O ciel!

CHORUS

She's off to Paris!   Elle est partie!

LESCAUT
(*furious*)

But it's a case of family honour!   Mais c'est l'honneur de la famille!

INNKEEPER
(*pointing to Guillot*)

She took his lordship's carriage too!   Dans la voiture de monsieur . . .

GUILLOT
(*to Lescaut who advances on him*)

No, that's enough!   Non! arrêtez! . . .

LESCAUT
(attempting to throw himself at Guillot)

You rogue!   Gredin!

GUILLOT
(freeing himself)

Let go! Let go!   Lâchez! Lâchez!

LESCAUT
(trying to recapture Guillot in spite of the innkeeper)

No, you have to learn your lesson!   Il faut que je châtie . . .

INNKEEPER AND CHORUS
(laughing)

Ah! ah! He's such a comic figure!   Ah! ah! la drôle de figure! —
Ah, what a trick for fate to play!   Vit-on jamais pareil malheur!

BRETIGNY
(coming out of the summer-house with the ladies)

What's this? Poor old Guillot! So your   Eh! quoi! Pauvre Guillot, votre belle est
sweet-heart has left you!   partie!

CHORUS
(laughing)

Oh what a sad misfortune . . .   Quelle mésaventure
For such a bold seducer too!   Pour un aussi grand séducteur!

GUILLOT

Now that's enough! I will take my revenge. Taisez-vous tous! . . . Je veux être vengé! . . .
That little bitch will suffer . . . this drunken   Et de cette perfide et de cet enragé!
brute will pay!

BRETIGNY, POUSSETTE, JAVOTTE, ROSETTE, INNKEEPER, TOWNSPEOPLE
(laughing)

Ah! ah! he's such a comic figure!   Ah! ah! la drôle de figure!
What a trick for fate to play!   Ah! quel malheur! ah! quel malheur!

LESCAUT

My God! Manon! Just wait until I find you Morbleu! Manon, vous me reverrez,
Then I'll really make you pay!   Et vous, petit, vous le paierez!

Everyone laughs, except Lescaut and Guillot.

Act Two

The apartment of Des Grieux and Manon in the rue Vivienne, Paris. The entrance door to the right, another door to the left. To the left, a little writing desk. A table close to the fireplace on the right. Very simple furnishings. At the back, a window with small panes looks onto the street.

Scene One. *Manon, Des Grieux, then a Servant. Des Grieux is seated before a little writing-desk. Manon comes up quietly behind him and tries to read what he is writing.* [10]

DES GRIEUX
(stopping and smiling reproachfully)

Manon! . . .   Manon! . . .

MANON
(gaily)

Do you not like feeling my cheek so gently   Avez-vous peur que mon visage frôle
Brushing against your own?   Votre visage?

DES GRIEUX
(smiling)

Ah, you're teasing Manon.   Indiscrète Manon! . . .

MANON

I stole a glance over your shoulder . . .   Oui, je lisais sur votre épaule . . .
I had to smile, seeing you write my name.   Et j'ai souri, voyant passer mon nom!

DES GRIEUX

I'm telling my father all about you: J'écris à mon père et je tremble
I hope my letter, which says all I feel,   Que cette lettre, où j'ai mis tout mon cœur,
    Won't upset him.   Ne l'irrite . . .

MANON

Are you afraid?   Vous avez peur?

DES GRIEUX

Yes, Manon, I'm afraid.   Oui, Manon, j'ai très peur . . .

MANON

Then come! Let us read it together.   Eh bien! il faut relire ensemble . . .

DES GRIEUX

Yes, you are right, Manon, I agree.   Oui, c'est cela, ensemble relisons!

MANON
(reading, simply)

'And her name is Manon, fresh as a flower   'On l'appelle Manon: elle eut hier seize
    in May.   ans.
'In her all charms unite . . . youthful grace   'En elle tout séduit . . . la beauté, la jeunesse,
    and an exquisite beauty.
'She has always such sweet things to say,   'La grâce; nulle voix n'a de plus doux
                                                      accents,
'Every glance is so charming and always so   'Nul regard, plus de charme avec plus de
    tender.'   tendresse . . .'

DES GRIEUX
(ardently)

Every glance is so charming and always so   Nul regard plus de charme avec plus de
    tender.   tendresse!

MANON
(looking up)

Is it true? Well, how can I say?   Est-ce vrai? Moi, je n'en sais rien;

61

But I know that you are in love.

(tenderly)

Mais je sais que vous m'aimez bien!

DES GRIEUX
(with spirit)

I, in love? . . . Manon . . . I adore you!

Vous aimer? . . . Manon . . . je t'adore!

MANON
(freeing herself)

Come on, Monsieur, back to the letter.

Allons . . . Monsieur, lisons encore! . . .

DES GRIEUX
(reading)

'Like a bird in the Spring, she delights in the sun
'And her spirit reaches outward
'Seeking life, begging it to possess her,
'Her lips are parted, seeming to call
'To the sweet scented breezes that gently caress her.'

'Comme l'oiseau qui suit en tous lieux le printemps,
'Sa jeune âme à la vie
'Sa jeune âme est ouverte sans cesse;
'Sa lèvre en fleur sourit et parle par instants
'Au zéphyr parfumé qui passe et la caresse!'

MANON
(repeating)

To the sweet scented breezes that gently caress her.

Au zéphyr parfumé qui passe et la caresse!

(speaking pensively)

Isn't it enough for you that we love each other?

Il ne te suffit pas alors de nous aimer?

DES GRIEUX
(warmly)

No, I want you to be my wife!

Non! Je veux que tu sois ma femme!

MANON
(warmly)

Do you really want that?

Tu le veux? . . .

DES GRIEUX

With all my soul!

Je le veux, et de toute mon âme!

MANON

Then kiss me chevalier!

Embrasse-moi donc, chevalier!

(They embrace.)

Now you must go and deliver the letter.

Et va porter ta lettre.

DES GRIEUX

Yes, I must.

Oui, je cours la porter!

He goes quickly to the door and stops, his eye caught by a bouquet near the fireplace.

DES GRIEUX
(disturbed)

That's a very beautiful bouquet!
Who sent these flowers?

Voilà des fleurs qui sont fort belles,
D'où te vient ce bouquet, Manon?

MANON
(with animation)

I don't know.

Je ne sais pas.

DES GRIEUX
(gravely)

You don't know?

Comment, tu ne sais pas?

MANON
(laughing)

It's not worth quarrelling over!

(with a feigned indifference)

Beau motif de querelles!

Somebody threw them up from the street,
And it was so pretty I kept it . . . I didn't think
It would make you jealous!

Par la fenêtre, on l'a lancé d'en bas . . .
Comme il était joli, je l'ai gardé . . . Je pense
Que tu n'est pas jaloux?

DES GRIEUX
(*tenderly*)

No, I promise
I have no doubts about your heart.

Non, je puis te jurer
Que je n'ai de ton cœur aucune défiance.

MANON

And you're right, because it belongs entirely
to you.

Et tu fais bien! Ce cœur est à toi tout entier!

(*An uproar of voices is heard outside.*)

DES GRIEUX

Who can be making all that noise?

Qui donc se permet un pareil tapage?

THE MAID
(*entering, bewildered*)

There are two guardsmen downstairs,
making a terrible scene.
One of them says he's a relation of yours,
Madam.

Deux gardes du corps sont là qui font rage!

L'un se dit le parent de madame . . .

MANON
(*relieved*)

Lescaut! . . .
It's Lescaut! . . .
C'est Lescaut!

Lescaut! . . .

MAID
(*in a low voice to Manon, quickly*)

The other one . . . is . . . let's keep our voices
down, . . .
The other one is an admirer of yours . . .
The rich tax collector who lives nearby . . .

L'autre c'est . . . ne parlons pas trop haut,

L'autre, c'est quelqu'un qui vous aime,
Ce fermier général qui loge près d'ici . . .

MANON
(*in a low voice, moved*)

Monsieur de Brétigny? . . .

Monsieur de Brétigny? . . .

MAID
(*in a low voice*)

Monsieur de Brétigny.

Monsieur de Brétigny.

DES GRIEUX
(*as the uproar increases*)

This is really too much! I'm going to see for
myself.

Cela devient trop fort et je vais voir moi-
même . . .

(*As he goes to the door, it opens.*)

Scene Two. *The same. Enter Brétigny in the costume of a guardsman and Lescaut.*

LESCAUT
(*brusquely*)

The two turtle doves:
So I've caught you at last.

Enfin, les amoureux,
Je vous tiens tous les deux!

BRETIGNY

Now don't be hard Lescaut! They're young
and so impulsive!

Soyez clément, Lescaut, songez à leur
jeunesse!

LESCAUT
(*insolently to Des Grieux*)

Quite a trick that you played! You slipped
away so neatly,
You cunning rascal.

Vous m'avez, l'autre jour, brûlé la politesse,

Monsieur le drôle!

DES GRIEUX
(with animation)

Now wait! You must be more polite!	Hé! là! parlez plus doucement!

LESCAUT
(ironically)

Be more polite!	Plus doucement!

DES GRIEUX
(calm and threatening)

Yes, more polite!	Plus doucement!

LESCAUT

I'm nearly stunned with surprise at his swagger!	C'est à tomber foudroyé sur la place!
I'm thirsting to avenge a point of family honour,	J'arrive pour venger l'honneur de notre race,
I'm here to seek redress, I've come to punish wrong,	Je suis le redresseur, je suis le châtiment,
And I am then told off because I'm not polite!	Et c'est à moi qu'on dit de parler doucement!

BRETIGNY

Please be calm!	Contiens-toi!

LESCAUT
(almost spoken)

You rogue!	Coquin!

BRETIGNY

Please be calm!	Retiens-toi!

DES GRIEUX

All right! I'm going to give you a thrashing!	C'est bien! Je vais vous couper les oreilles!

LESCAUT
(to Brétigny, pretending not to have understood)

What? What did he say?	Hein? Qu'est-ce qu'il dit? . . .

BRETIGNY
(laughing, to Lescaut)

He's going to give you a thrashing.	Qu'il va vous couper les oreilles!

LESCAUT

Why does he shout in this insolent fashion?	Vit-on jamais insolences pareilles?
Does he mean it?	Il menace . . .

BRETIGNY

I think he does . . .	Ça m'en a l'air . . .

LESCAUT

Now by God! Now by hell!	Par la mort! par l'enfer . . .
You rogue!	Coquin!

MANON

Ah, chevalier, I'm so afraid!	[11] Ah! chevalier, je meurs d'effroi!
I realise that I am guilty!	Je le sais bien, je suis coupable!
Look after me!	Veillez sur moi, oh, chevalier!
Ah! We're done for!	Ah! c'en est fait!
His angry shouting overwhelms me!	Son regard courroucé m'accable.
I'm so afraid! I'm so afraid!	Ah! chevalier, veillez sur moi!

DES GRIEUX

O Manon, do not be afraid!	O Manon, soyez sans effroi!
Depend on me! I am the only one who's guilty!	Seul de nous deux, je suis coupable,

64

Depend on me!   Comptez sur moi!
My dearest love, don't be afraid.   O cher amour! Ne tremblez pas!
I'm sure he'll soon be less unfriendly.   Il sera bientôt plus traitable;
  Manon depend on me!   O Manon, comptez sur moi!

LESCAUT
(alternately to Brétigny and Des Grieux)

De Brétigny! Don't let me fight!   Retenez-moi! retenez-moi!
  Scoundrel!   Drôle!
If I lay hands on him I'll kill him.   Je sais de quoi je suis capable!
I'm like a lion when I'm angry   Quand il faut punir un coupable!
  Don't let me fight! Don't let me fight!   Retenez-moi! retenez-moi!

BRETIGNY
(restraining him)

Please be calm Lescaut!   Contiens-toi, Lescaut,
Their remorse overwhelms them! Look!   Vois! le remords les accable!
What a pair! They are guilty!   Chacun d'eux est coupable;
  Oh come! You must forgive them!   Allons, de l'indulgence,
    Please be calm Lescaut!   Contiens-toi, Lescaut, retiens-toi!
(interposing)
Lescaut, this display is excessive!   Lescaut, vous montrez trop de zèle!
Compose yourself and state your case.   Expliquez-vous plus posément.

LESCAUT
(self-importantly)

Right! I agree!   Soit, j'y consens.
(to Des Grieux)
I find my cousin   Mademoiselle
Here with you, and since I'm asked to be   Est ma cousine, et je venais très poliment ...
polite ...

DES GRIEUX
(still threatening)

Yes, be polite!   Très poliment?

LESCAUT

That's what I said ...   Très poliment,
I always am very polite ...   Oui, je venais très poliment
Tell me, Monsieur, I do not seek a quarrel ...   Dire: Monsieur, sans vous chercher
     querelle
Just answer yes, or answer no!   Répondez: Oui, répondez: Non,
Do you intend to wed Manon?   Voulez-vous épouser Manon?

BRETIGNY AND LESCAUT

It's all quite clear   Le chose est claire;
  As clear as day,   Entre lurons
  I think you'd say   Et bons garçons
And that's the way we should treat it.   C'est ainsi qu'on traite une affaire!

BRETIGNY
(laughing, to Des Grieux)

Now tell us if that's what you want.   Eh bien, êtes-vous satisfait?

DES GRIEUX
(laughing)

I own I'm completely defeated.   Ma foi, je n'ai plus de colère,
Your frankness is just what I like.   Et votre franchise me plaît.
(to Lescaut)
I have written this to my father.   Je venais d'écrire à mon père ...
(showing the letter)
Before I seal and send it off,   Avant qu'on y mette un cachet,
I'd be obliged if you would read it.   Vous lirez bien ceci, j'espère ...

LESCAUT
(taking the letter)

If you wish! The light is so poor ...   Volontiers! Mais, voici le soir ...

If we're to read, why don't we go   Allons, tous deux, pour y mieux voir,

(intentionally taking Des Grieux aside from them)

Over there, just there by the window,   Nous placer près de la fenêtre,

And then we can go through your letter.   Et là nous lirons votre lettre . . .

Lescaut has gone upstage with Des Grieux. Brétigny is near Manon. [12]

MANON
(to Brétigny, furtively)

Why are you here . . . and in this strange   Venir ici sous un déguisement! . . .
disguise?

BRÉTIGNY
(to Manon, furtively)

Do not be cross!   Vous m'en voulez?

MANON

Have you gone mad?   Certainement . . .
You know well he's the one I worship.   Vous savez que c'est lui que j'aime!

BRÉTIGNY

I am here only to give you warning: J'ai voulu vous avertir, moi-même,
You should know there's a plan to kidnap   Que ce soir de chez vous on compte
him tonight . . .   l'enlever . . .

MANON

Tonight?   Ce soir?

BRÉTIGNY

His father gave the order.   Par ordre de son père!

MANON
(surprised, with feeling)

His father gave the order!   Par ordre de son père!

BRÉTIGNY

Yes, tonight men will call here, they will   Oui, ce soir, ici même on viendra
drag him away . . .   l'arracher . . .

MANON
(taking a step)

Ah! Then I shall warn Des Grieux.   Ah! je saurai bien empêcher . . .

BRÉTIGNY
(stopping her)

If you speak out you will regret it,   Prévenez-le, c'est la misère
Both he and you,   Pour lui, pour vous . . .

(in a low voice, very near her)

but if you don't speak out,   Ne le prévenez pas,
A lifetime of riches and pleasure   Et c'est la fortune, au contraire,
Will soon be yours.   Qui vous attend . . .

MANON
(with animation, fearfully)

Don't let him hear!   Parlez plus bas!
I can't!   Jamais!

LESCAUT
(accentuating each syllable accusingly)

'And her name is Manon,   'On l'appelle Manon,
'She's like a flower in May.   'Elle eut hier seize ans . . .
'In her all charms unite.'   'En elle tout séduit!'

(changing his tone, laughing)

I am moved by his words.   Que ces mots sont touchants!

Ah! Lescaut, truly I adore her!	Ah! Lescaut, c'est que je l'adore,
I want to live my whole life for her.	Laissez-moi vous le dire encore!

LESCAUT

You'll marry her?	Vous l'épousez?

(reading)

'She's like a bird in Spring, she delights the sun.'	'Comme l'oiseau qui suit le printemps, en tous le printemps!'
How poetic is love!	O poésie! amour! . . .

(reading)

'To the sweet scented breezes . . .' How poetic!	'Sa jeune âme à la vie . . .' Poésie!
You'll marry her. Indeed!	M'enchante, par ma foi!

BRETIGNY

Manon! Manon!	Manon! Manon!

MANON

Don't let him hear!	Parlez plus bas!

BRETIGNY

Manon! Come seize hold of this moment,	Manon, voici l'heure prochaine
For it can set you free.	De votre liberté!
Manon! I swear I see you reigning,	Manon, bientôt vous serez reine,
Reigning as queen of love!	Reine par la beauté!

MANON
(aside)

I'm filled with doubt, I don't know why.	Quel doute étrange et quel tourment!
I don't know how to answer!	Dans mon cœur troublé quel délire!
I feel such longing yet I'm afraid.	Quel doute étrange et quel tourment!
I'm so afraid, for my heart has now to decide!	Ah! quel tourment, pour mon cœur troublé!
Ah, please go! Ah, now go!	Ah! partez! ah! partez!

LESCAUT

All agreed! Nothing could be better!	C'est parfait, on ne peut mieux dire
With all my heart I wish you well.	Et je vous fais mon compliment!

(to Manon)

Dear cousin,	Cousine,

(to Des Grieux)

and you, dear friend,	et vous, cousin,

(with self-importance)

how I honour your feelings!	je vous rends mon estime!

(to both of them)

Now we'll shake hands, for it would be unfeeling	Prenez ma main, car ce serait un crime
To hold you to account. Young friends . . . I bless you both!	De vous tenir rigueur. Enfants, je vous bénis . . .

(with tenderness so exaggerated as to be comical)

I'm weeping tears of joy . . .	Les larmes . . . le bonheur . . .

(aside to Brétigny, changing his tone)

Shall we go?	Partons-nous?

BRETIGNY
(changing his tone)

After you . . .	Je vous suis!

LESCAUT AND BRETIGNY

It's all quite clear,	La chose est claire!
As clear as day,	Entre lurons
And that's the way	Et bons garçons,
That we should treat it!	C'est ainsi qu'on traite une affaire!

They go out.

Scene Three. *Manon, Des Grieux, the Maid.*

MANON
(pensively, to herself)

| In my heart I'm afraid. | Dans mon cœur quel tourment ... |

DES GRIEUX
(happily to himself)

| God grant that tomorrow will bring me | Puisse du bonheur où j'aspire |
| The happiness too long delayed. | Le jour se lever souriant! ... |

Enter the Maid with a lamp.

DES GRIEUX
(speaking)

| What is it? | Que nous veut-on? |

MAID

| It's suppertime | C'est l'heure du souper, |
| Monsieur. | Monsieur. |

DES GRIEUX
(smiling)

| So it is, and I still haven't | [0] C'est vrai pourtant. Et je n'ai pas encore |
| Taken my letter. | Porté ma lettre! |

The Maid spreads the tablecloth for supper.

MANON

| Go and take it now. | Eh bien, va la porter! |

DES GRIEUX
(undecided)

| Manon ... | Manon! |

MANON

| What is it? | Après? |

DES GRIEUX
(slowly and tenderly)

| I love you, I adore you. | Je t'aime, je t'adore! |
| But ... do you love me? | Et toi, dis, m'aimes-tu? |

MANON

| Yes, my dear chevalier, | Oui, mon cher chevalier ... |
| I love you. | Je t'aime ... |

DES GRIEUX
(in a reproachful tone)

| In that case you ought to promise me ... | Tu devrais, en ce cas, me promettre ... |

MANON

| What? | Quoi? |

DES GRIEUX
(changing his tone)

| Nothing ... Nothing at all. | Rien du tout! ... Je vais porter ma lettre! |

Exit.

Scene Four. *Manon.*

MANON
(deeply troubled)

And now! If I go ...	Allons! ... il le faut! ...
It's for his sake!	Pour lui-même!
My dearest chevalier ... I know I really love him,	Mon pauvre chevalier! ... Oh! Oui, c'est lui que j'aime!

68

Even so, I cannot decide!	Et pourtant, j'hésite aujourd'hui!
No, no! I'm no longer worthy of him!	Non! non! je ne suis plus digne de lui!
I'm drawn by a voice that acclaims me,	J'entends cette voix qui m'entraîne
But in spite of myself!	Contre ma volonté:
Manon, I see you reigning,	"Manon, tu seras reine,
Reigning fair queen of love!	"Reine par la beauté!"

(with self reproach; then weakly)

I'm so weak and so fickle ... Why should I feel like this?	Je ne suis que faiblesse et que fragilité! ...
Ah, against my will I feel sad and wretched ...	Ah! malgré moi je sens couler mes larmes.
Our happy life is past and done; [10]	Devant ces rêves effacés!
What's in store, will it be so precious,	L'avenir aura-t-il les charmes
Like the sweet days that now are gone?	De ces beaux jours déjà passés?

(Little by little Manon has approached the table where the meal is spread.)

Farewell, our happy little table, [14]	Adieu, notre petite table
This is where we sat every day!	Qui nous réunit si souvent!
Farewell, farewell our happy life together.	Adieu, notre petite table,
A world of our own he would say!	Si grande pour nous cependant!

(with a sad smile)

We sat as close as we were able,	On tient, c'est inimaginable,
His arm around me ... that was his way!	Si peu de place en se serrant!

A single glass was all we needed	Un même verre était le nôtre,
And in the glass I'd leave a kiss,	Chacun de nous, quand il buvait,
And he would find it and taste it.	Y cherchait les lèvres de l'autre ...
Ah, my poor friend, how well you love!	Ah! Pauvre ami, comme il m'aimait! ...
Farewell, our happy life together.	Adieu ... notre petite table.

(with a sob)

Farewell!	Adieu!

(hearing Des Grieux, aside, with animation)

He's back! I look so pale. I hope he doesn't see!	C'est lui! Que ma pâleur ne me trahisse pas!

Scene Five. Manon, Des Grieux.

DES GRIEUX
(with spirit)

Dearest Manon, now we're alone together.	Enfin, Manon, nous voilà seuls ensemble!

(He comes closer to her.)

What's this? You're crying?	Eh quoi? ... des larmes?

MANON

No!   Non!

DES GRIEUX

My love, you are trembling!	Si fait, ta main tremble ...

MANON
(forcing a smile)

Our supper will be cold ...	Voici notre repas.

DES GRIEUX

You're right! I'm so excited ...	C'est vrai, ma tête est folle!
But joy is such a fleeting thing,	Mais le bonheur est passager,
A summer bird upon the wing,	Et le ciel l'a fait si léger
I'm always frightened it will vanish!	Qu'on a toujours peur qu'il s'envole!
Our supper.	A table!

MANON

Our supper!   A table!

DES GRIEUX

Enchanting hour	Instant charmant
When we sit in the twilight,	Où la crainte fait trève,
Just the two of us, quite alone!	Où nous sommes deux seulement!
Ah, Manon, as I walked I lost myself in day-dreams.	Tiens, Manon, en marchant, je viens de faire un rêve.

69

MANON
(aside, bitterly)

Alas! I spend my life in daydreams!   Hélas! qui ne fait pas de rêve?

DES GRIEUX
(to Manon, intimately)

When I close my eyes I see [15]	En fermant les yeux, je vois
So clear a beautiful haven,	Là-bas une humble retraite,
Just a simple cottage,	Une maisonnette
Small and white, among the trees.	Toute blanche au fond des bois!
Beneath the shady branches,	Sous ses tranquilles ombrages
Clear streams gently rippling by,	Les clairs et joyeux ruisseaux,
Leaves are mirrored in the waters,	Où se mirent les feuillages,
Birds are singing in the sky!	Chantent avec les oiseaux!
It will be like heaven! Ah! no!	C'est le paradis! . . . Oh non!
Heaven now is sad and empty	Tout est là triste et morose,
And heaven never could tempt me,	Car il y manque une chose,
Without my dear Manon!	Il y faut encore Manon!

MANON
(softly)

You are dreaming, it couldn't happen!   C'est un rêve, une folie!

DES GRIEUX

That is where we'll be content.   Non! Là sera notre vie!
Ah, please say yes, my Manon!   Si tu le veux, ô Manon,

Knocking is heard at the door.

MANON
(aside)

Oh God! So soon!   Oh ciel! déjà!

DES GRIEUX

Who's that?   Quelqu'un!
(gaily)
We don't need company this evening.   Il ne faut pas de trouble fête . . .
(rising)
I'll deal with whoever is there.   Je vais renvoyer l'importun.
(smiling)
I won't be long!   Et je reviens.

MANON
(troubled)

Farewell!   Adieu!

DES GRIEUX
(astonished)

Manon?   Comment! . . .

MANON
(with embarrassment and suppressed emotion)

No! Don't go away!   Non! Je ne veux pas! . . .

DES GRIEUX
(insisting)

Why not?   Pourquoi?

MANON

Don't go near the door, I entreat you!   Tu n'ouvriras pas cette porte!
I want to stay in your arms.   Je veux rester dans tes bras!

DES GRIEUX
(gently freeing himself)

My love! Let me go! Are you frightened?   Enfant! . . . laisse-moi . . . que t'importe!

MANON

No!   Non!

DES GRIEUX

Well then!   Allons! . . .

MANON

Stay with me here!   Je ne veux pas! . . .

DES GRIEUX

A stranger's coach . . . That's very odd!   Quelque inconnu! . . . C'est singulier!
I'll send him on his way both firmly and   Je le congédierai d'une façon polie,
  politely . . .
When I'm back we will laugh and guess   Je reviens, nous rirons tous deux de ta folie!
  why you were frightened!

He kisses her and leaves. There is the sound of a struggle. Manon runs to the window. The
rumbling of a carriage is heard.

MANON

My poor chevalier!   Mon pauvre chevalier!

Manon is overcome by grief. Slow curtain.

Victoria de los Angeles as Manon and André Turp as Des Grieux in Act Two at Covent
Garden in 1960 (Royal Opera House Archives)

71

Act Three

First Tableau. The main walk in the Cours la Reine on a public holiday. On the right, a notice for a ball. Between the great trees are the little shops of every sort of tradesman: dress-makers, toy-sellers, jugglers, song-sellers etc.; there is a lot of activity as the curtain rises; the shopkeepers pursue the passers-by — nobility and townspeople — offering them different things. At the back one can see the banks of the Seine and the dome of the Invalides.

Scene One. *Chorus, Milliners, Vendors, Cooks, Townspeople.*

MILLINERS, DRESS-MAKERS

See my slippers, sewn with flowers,	Voyez! mules à fleurettes,
Pretty shawls and silken hoods.	Fichus et coqueluchons,
Petticoats and caps and collars!	Bonnets, paniers, collerettes,
Gauze and lawn and stylish muffs!	Gaze, linon et manchons!

TRADESMAN

Buy my elixir of life!	Elixir pour l'estomac!

TRADESWOMAN

Rouge and patches, cuffs and ruffles,	Rouge, mouches et manchettes,
Feathers, plumes and slender aigrettes!	Plumes et fines aigrettes!

TRADESMAN

Powder and tobacco here!	Poudre, râpes à tabac!

SONG-SELLER

Come buy, come buy my songs!	Achetez-moi mes chansons!

COOK

Buy yourself a lovely present.	Il est temps qu'on se régale,
As a cook I have no rival!	Ma cuisine est sans égale!

SONG-SELLER

Come buy, come buy my songs!	Achetez-mois mes chansons!

GROUP OF TRADESMEN

Buy your tickets for the lottery!	Billets pour la loterie,
Ribbons, walking sticks and hats.	Rubans, cannes et chapeaux!
Every kind of sweet and pastry!	Bonbons et pâtisserie,
Toys and balls and tops and whips!	Jouets, balles et sabots!

CHORUS

Today is Cours la Reine.	[16]	C'est fête au Cours-la-Reine!
Let us laugh, let us drink,		On y rit, on y boit,
Long life unto our King!		A la santé du Roi!
Long life unto our King!		Pendant une semaine.

Poussette and Javotte come out of the dance-hall. Two young men who seem to be looking for someone in the crowd see them, and, at a signal from the two girls, run to meet them. Soon afterwards Rosette enters.

POUSSETTE, JAVOTTE

How delightful, how diverting!	La charmante promenade!
Sweet adventures may arise . . .	Ah! que ce séjour est doux!
Just the place to chose for flirting,	Que c'est bon une escapade,
Far from jealous lovers' eyes!	Loin des regards d'un jaloux!

POUSSETTE

Then we're agreed!	C'est entendu!

JAVOTTE

Now don't forget!	Tenez-vous bien! . . .

72

ROSETTE

A hasty word and we must sever ...	Un mot pourrait nous compromettre!

JAVOTTE

My heart is yours, and yours forever!	Mon cœur veut bien tout vous pro- mettre ...

POUSSETTE, JAVOTTE AND ROSETTE

But not a word to old Guillot!	Mais que Guillot n'en sache rien! ...

Poussette and Javotte return to the dance-hall, Rosette moves away. Reprise of the Chorus.

Scene Two. *The same, Lescaut, forcing his way through the crowd.*

TRADESMEN
(following Lescaut)

Look here, monsieur! Try this monsieur! Monsieur, you simply have to make your choice!	Tenez, monsieur! Prenez, monsieur! Prenez! Choisissez!

LESCAUT

My choice? I'll take this ...   Choisir, et pourquoi?
And that! Give me another!   Donnez! Donnez encore!
Today I buy it all!   Ce soir j'achète tout!
Beauty rules and I serve no other.   C'est pour la beauté que j'adore,
I see delight on every stall.   Je m'en rapporte à votre goût.

He takes all the objects offered to him and pays everyone.

Where's the fun in living cheaply [17]	A quoi bon l'économie
When your dice is in your hand	Quand on a trois dés en main,
And your cards you've sharply scanned	Et que l'on sait le chemin
In the Hotel Transylvania?	De l'hôtel de Transylvanie!

TRADESMEN

Look here monsieur. Try this! Try this!	Tenez! monsieur, tenez! Prenez!

LESCAUT
(his arms full of purchases)

Now that's enough!	Assez! assez!

(with feeling)

O Rosalinda!	O Rosalinde,
I'd need to have the gifts of Pindar	Il me faudrait gravir le Pinde,
To sing of you as you deserve!	Pour te chanter comme il convient!
Sultanas from the hills of India	Que sont les sultanes de l'Inde
And fair Armida and Clorinda,	Et les Armide et les Clorinde
Next to you, have they beauty? No!	Près de toi, que sont-elles? Rien,
Not at all! O my Rosalinda!	Rien du tout, ô ma Rosalinde!
Enough! On my life.	Choisir, non ma foi!
Where's the fun in living cheaply [17]	A quoi bon l'économie
When your dice is in your hand	Quand on a trois dés en main
And your cards you've sharply scanned	Et que l'on sait le chemin
In the Hotel Transylvania?	De l'hôtel de Transylvanie!
Come to me! You beauties, come to me!	Approchez, belles, approchez ...
I offer you a jewelled ring for one embrace!	J'offre un bijou pour deux baisers ...

Exit Lescaut. Bustle of the crowd.

Scene Three. *Guillot, Poussette, Javotte and Rosette come out of the dance-hall. Dance music in the distance.*

GUILLOT
(seeing them)

My dear Poussette!	Bonjour Poussette!

POUSSETTE
(crying out)

Ah Guillot!	Ah! ciel!

73

GUILLOT

What's this, Javotte!   Bonjour Javotte!

JAVOTTE
(*crying out*)

Oh God!   Ah! Dieu!

Poussette and Javotte run away.

GUILLOT

You too Rosette!   Bonjour Rosette!

ROSETTE
(*crying out, she runs away*)

Ah!   Ah!

GUILLOT

Devil take them!   Par la morbleu!
They've given me the slip. Little slut! Bitch!   Elles me plantent là! Coquine! Péronnelle!
And I brought all three of them here because   Et j'en avais pris trois pourtant il me
                                semblait
I thought if one of them deceived me   Pouvoir compter, si l'une me trompait,
I'd have one of the others to be nice to me!   Qu'une autre au moins serait fidèle.
Frailty, thy name is woman!   La femme est, je l'avoue, un méchant
                                animal!

BRETIGNY
(*who has entered and heard these last words*)

Not bad Guillot,   Pas mal, Guillot, ce mot-là n'est pas mal!
But not very original!   Mais il n'est pas de vous!
(*Guillot looks at him furiously.*)
Good God, what a gloomy face!   Dieu! quel sombre visage!
Has Javotte   Dame Javotte, je le gage,
Been leading you a dance?   Vous aura fait des traits ...

GUILLOT
(*angrily*)

It's all over with Javotte.   Javotte? c'est fini!

BRETIGNY

And Poussette?   Et ... Poussette?

GUILLOT

All over with her too!   Poussette aussi!

BRETIGNY
(*with irony*)

So you're free? Guillot, you wouldn't try   Vous voilà libre alors! Guillot, je vous en
                              prie,
To take Manon from me, would you?   N'allez pas m'enlever Manon!

GUILLOT

Take Manon?   Vous enlever? ...

BRETIGNY
(*beseeching ironically*)

No! Swear to me that you won't.   Non, jurez-moi que non!

GUILLOT

How could you think it of me!   Laissons cette plaisanterie!
By the way,   Mais dites-moi, mon cher, on m'a conté
Talking of Manon, is it true she wanted you   A propos de Manon, que vous ayant prié
To bring the Opera ballet to dance   De faire venir l'Opéra chez elle,
At her house and that despite all her tears   Vous avez, en dépit des larmes de la belle,
You said no?   Répondu non?

BRÉTIGNY

Quite true; that is exactly What happened!	C'est très vrai; la nouvelle Est exacte!

GUILLOT

You intrigue me . . . Well I must leave you For a while. Will you excuse me!	Il suffit! Souffrez que je vous quitte Pour un instant; mais je reviendrai vite!
(He leaves rubbing his hands together and humming.)	
Dig a dig a don. One day he will lose his Manon.	Et dig et dig et don, On te la prendra, ta Manon!

Scene Four. *Brétigny. Promenaders and vendors return, then Manon.*

CHORUS
[18]

The fashionable ladies! The pleasure loving ladies! Ruling with their arts Many rich men's hearts!	Voici les élégantes, Les belles indolentes, Maîtresses des cœurs, Aux regards vainqueurs!

Enter Manon accompanied by Brétigny and several young noblemen.

PROMENADERS, TRADESWOMEN
(to each other)

But look, look at this goddess! Can she be less than a duchess?	Quelle est cette princesse? C'est au moins une duchesse!

OTHER TRADESWOMEN
(to the promenaders)

What! Don't you even know her name? It's Manon! That's the lovely Manon!	Eh! ne savez-vous pas son nom? C'est Manon! C'est la belle Manon!

CHORUS

The fashionable ladies! The pleasure loving ladies!	Voici les élégantes Les belles indolentes!

Whilst this is going on Brétigny has advanced with some noblemen who are his friends and has helped Manon descend from her sedan-chair.

BRÉTIGNY

You're so lovely Manon!	Ravissante Manon!

MANON

How do I look today?	Suis-je gentille ainsi?

BRÉTIGNY AND NOBLEMEN

We adore you! A goddess! A goddess!	Adorable, divine! divine!

MANON

Is it true? You are kind.	Est-ce vrai? Grand merci!
(coquettishly)	
I must be the kindest of creatures To allow you to gaze on my beautiful features!	Je consens, vu que je suis bonne, A laisser admirer ma charmante personne . . .
(with impertinence and gaiety)	
I rule as the queen of the land. The whole world crowds round me acclaiming; They bow low and kiss my hand, At beauty's command I am reigning!	Je marche sur tous les chemins Aussi bien qu'une souveraine; On s'incline, on baise ma main, Car par la beauté je suis reine!
No-one's horses dare race so fast. Each day something new and exciting: They take their hats off as they pass: I am lovely and I am so happy!	Mes chevaux courent à grands pas; Devant ma vie aventureuse, Les grands s'avancent chapeau bas; Je suis belle, je suis heureuse!

The town blossoms when I go by!	Autour de moi, tout doit fleurir!
I love life and not what comes after!	Je vais à tout ce qui m'attire!
And if Manon should ever have to die,	Et si Manon devait jamais mourir,
The last you'd hear from her would be a shout of laughter!	Ce cerait, mes amis, dans un éclat de rire!
Ah! ah! ah!	Ah! ah! ah! ...

BRETIGNY AND NOBLEMEN

Bravo! Bravo! Manon!	Bravo! Bravo! Manon!

Gavotte.

MANON

Venus is calling, I must obey her,	Obéissons quand leur voix appelle
Sharing tender love with you, or you, or you.	Aux tendres amours, toujours, toujours, toujours.
Don't ever count the days, let love possess you all life through,	Tant que vous êtes belle, usez sans les compter vos jours,
All life through.	Tous vos jours.
Ah, in delay there lies no plenty,	Profitons bien de la jeunesse,
What's to come is still unsure.	Des jours qu'amène le printemps;
Then come and kiss me sweet and twenty,	Aimons, rions, chantons sans cesse,
For youth's a stuff will not endure.	Nous n'avons encore que vingt ans.

BRETIGNY AND NOBLEMEN

In delay there lies no plenty	Profitons bien de la jeunesse,
Then come and kiss me five and twenty,	Aimons, rions, chantons sans cesse,
For youth's a stuff will not endure!	Nous n'avons encore que vingt ans!

MANON

A heart, alas, can never be faithful.	Le cœur hélas! le plus fidèle,
Love may only last one day.	Oublie en un jour l'amour,
Then youth will spread his wings	Et la jeunesse ouvrant son aile
To fly away, to fly	A disparu sans retour,
Far away!	Sans retour.

Reprise of the refrain.

MANON
(to Brétigny)

Wait for me here, there's a bracelet I want ...	Et maintenant restez seul un instant;
I just can't resist the temptation.	Je veux faire ici quelque emplette.

BRÉTIGNY
(gracefully)

When you go shadows fall over this bright occasion!	Avec vous disparaît tout l'éclat de la fête!
You're so lovely Manon!	Ravissante Manon!

MANON

Oh what a phrase!	Une fadeur! ...
That was gallantly said!	C'est du dernier galant!
Some great poet for sure, gave you that inspiration!	On n'est pas grand seigneur sans être un peu poète!

Manon goes towards the booths upstage, followed by some inquisitive people, who gradually disperse.

Scene Five. *Brétigny, the Count, Manon.*

BRETIGNY

Comte des Grieux if I'm not mistaken.	Je ne me trompe pas? le comte Des Grieux!

COUNT

Monsieur de Brétigny?	Monsieur de Brétigny ...

Adele Leigh as Manon with Otakar Kraus as De Brétigny at Covent Garden in 1955
(Royal Opera House Archives)

BRETIGNY

Your servant! You in Paris!
I can hardly believe my eyes.

Moi-même; c'est à peine
Si je puis en croire mes yeux! Vous, à
Paris?

COUNT

It's on my son's account that I'm here ...

C'est mon fils qui m'amène ...

BRETIGNY

The Chevalier?

Le chevalier! ...

COUNT

Chevalier no longer.
We must now call him Abbé Des Grieux.

Il n'est plus chevalier,
C'est l'abbé Des Grieux qu'à présent il faut
dire ...

Manon has approached while pretending to be talking with a tradesman.

MANON
(*aside*)

Des Grieux!

Des Grieux!

BRETIGNY

Your son? Is it possible?

Abbé! lui! comment ...

COUNT

Heaven has called him.
He intends to take holy orders.
He is at St Sulpice, and this evening

He is to preach at the Sorbonne.

Le Ciel l'attire!
Dans les ordres, il veut entrer;
Il est à Saint-Sulpice, et, ce soir en
Sorbonne
Il prononce un discours.

Manon withdraws after having heard these words.

BRETIGNY
(*smiling*)

Abbé!
What an astonishing change!

Abbé! cela m'étonne;
Un pareil changement! ...

COUNT
(*also smiling*)

You brought the change about
When you caused him to break off
His relationship with a certain person.

C'est vous qui l'avez fait,
En vous chargeant de briser net
L'amour qui l'attachait à certaine personne.

BRETIGNY
(*pointing out Manon upstage*)

Not so loud!

Plus bas! ...

COUNT

Is that the girl?

C'est elle? ...

BRETIGNY

Yes that's Manon!

Oui, c'est Manon.

COUNT
(*jokingly*)

She really is very beautiful.
I understand now why you
Took such an interest in my son's affairs.

Je devine alors la raison
Qui vous fit, avec tant de zèle,
Prendre les intérêts de mon fils ...

(*seeing Manon approaching*)
Mais, pardon

I think she wants to speak to you.

Elle veut vous parler ...

He bows and withdraws a little; aside.

[She is really very lovely!]

Elle est vraiment fort belle!

MANON
(to Brétigny)

My dear, I want
Another bracelet to match this . . .
And I can't find one anywhere.

Je voudrais, mon ami,
Avoir un bracelet pareil à celui-ci . . .
Je ne puis le trouver . . .

BRETIGNY

Leave it to me. I'll find one for you.

C'est bien, je vais moi-même . . .

Exit, bowing to the Count.

COUNT
(aside)

Charming! I see now why they all fall in
love with her.

Elle est charmante et je comprends qu'on
l'aime!

Scene Six. *Manon, the Count.*

MANON
(to the Count with embarrassment)

Monsieur . . . I was near-by . . . and I
heard what you said . . .
When one listens by chance . . . the secrets
one discovers . . .

Pardon . . . mais j'étais là . . . près de vous,
à deux pas . . .
J'entendais malgré moi . . . je suis très
curieuse . . .

COUNT
(smiling)

A very little sin in the life that we lead . . .

C'est un petit défaut . . . très petit ici-bas . . .

(bowing, wishing to withdraw)

Your servant!

Madame!

MANON
(approaching)

I think you spoke of a story of two lovers?

Il s'agissait d'une histoire . . . amoureuse?

COUNT
(astonished)

We did.

Mais oui . . .

MANON
(restraining her emotion)

That's what I thought.
I hope you will not be offended.
I think that this Abbé Des Grieux was in
love . . .
In love . . .

C'est que je crois . . .
Pardonnez-moi, je vous en prie . . .
Je crois que cet abbé . . . Des Grieux,
autrefois
Aimait . . .

COUNT

With whom?

Qui donc? . . .

MANON

She and I once were friendly.

Elle était mon amie . . .

COUNT

Ah! I see!

Ah! très bien! . . .

MANON
(with rising emotion)

How he loved! I only want to know . . .
Whether his reason conquered his
emotion . . .
Or whether his devotion
To her who betrayed him
Still lives in his heart. Dare I ask? I'm
afraid . . .

Il l'aimait, et je voudrais savoir
Si sa raison sortit victorieuse . . .
Et si, de l'oublieuse
Il a pu parvenir
A chasser de son cœur le cruel
souvenir? . . .

79

COUNT
(*lightly and with expression*)

Ah, the questions youth proposes!	Faut-il donc savoir tant de choses?
What becomes of a summer day,	Que deviennent les plus beaux jours,
Who stole our first love away	Où vont les premières amours,
And whither flies the scent of roses?	Où vole le parfum des roses?

MANON
(*aside*)

Dear God, make me strong, give me courage	Mon Dieu! Donnez-moi le courage
To ask him all I need to know.	De tout oser lui demander!

COUNT

Live your life, think about tomorrow.	Ignorer n'est-il pas plus sage,
Do not linger over what is past.	Au passé pourquoi s'attarder?

MANON

Just one more minute! Did it appear his heart was breaking?	Un mot encore!... A-t-il souffert de son absence?...
And does he ever speak her name?	Vous a-t-il dit parfois son nom?

COUNT
(*looking at her steadily*)

He shed all his tears without speaking.	Ses larmes coulaient en silence...

MANON
(*deeply moved*)

He didn't curse when he wept?	L'a-t-il maudite, en pleurant?...

COUNT

No!	Non!

MANON

He didn't say that she who cheated Had also loved?	Vous a-t-il dit que la parjure L'avait aimé?

COUNT
(*after hesitating a moment*)

His wound was healed and he retreated Inside himself!	Son cœur, guéri de sa blessure, S'est refermé!

MANON

But since then?	Mais depuis?...

COUNT
(*lightly and with a purpose*)

He made no more fuss and no more bother.	Il a fait ainsi que votre amie,
And I hope your friend did the same.	Ce que l'on doit faire ici-bas,
It wasn't serious, just a game...	Quand on est sage, n'est-ce pas?
He forgot her!	On oublie!

MANON
(*sadly, to herself*)

He forgot her!	On oublie!

The Count bows respectfully and withdraws.

Scene Seven. *Manon, Brétigny, Guillot then Lescaut. Enter lords and ladies of fashion, promenaders, vendors, Brétigny and Guillot with some friends, then Lescaut.*

BRETIGNY

Answer me Guillot.	Répondez-moi, Guillot!

(*laughter*)

Never! He who laughs last,   Jamais! Mais rira bien
Laughs longest.   Qui rira le dernier!

BRETIGNY

Monsieur de Morfontaine,   Monsieur de Morfontaine,
I demand that you tell me everything! Vous allez tout me dire!

GUILLOT

I will tell you nothing!   A vous, mon ami, rien!
(turning to Manon)
Ah, but you, my queen!   Mais à vous, ô ma reine!

BRETIGNY

But I insist.   Plaît-il?

GUILLOT

Very well then — the dancers   Eh bien! oui . . . l'Opéra
You so desired to see shall   Que vous lui refusiez . . . le sera
Perform for you here at my expense. Dans un instant ici.

(a bustle in the crowd)

BRETIGNY
(to Guillot)

I surrender!   Je dois rendre les armes! . . .
(to Manon)
Manon you're sad!   Vous êtes triste?

MANON

No, no!   Oh! non!

BRETIGNY

I think I see tears.   On dirait que des larmes . . .

MANON

Nonsense!   Folie!

GUILLOT
(to Manon)

My dear Manon, come sit here if you please. Allons, Manon, approchez, s'il vous plaît:
(impressively)
They want to dance for you something On va danser pour vous notre nouveau
 entirely new!   ballet!
(to Lescaut)
Lescaut, come here!   Lescaut, venez!

LESCAUT
(very eagerly)

I am here at your service.   Je suis là pour vous plaire.

GUILLOT

Attend to everybody's needs.   Veillez . . . le tout est à mes frais,
It's all at my expense for all these people. A ce qu'on donne à boire au populaire.
(taking out his purse)
How much?   Combien? . . .

LESCAUT
(taking the purse and going out)

We'll settle later on!   Nous compterons après! . . .

NOBLEMEN AND TOWNSPEOPLE

What a splendid treat!   Voici l'Opéra!
Here they are! The dancers are here! L'Opéra! Voici l'Opéra!

Wonderful! Let's raise a cheer!	Tout Paris en parlera!
A new ballet soon will appear!	C'est le ballet de l'Opéra!
It is a feast to please a sovereign!	C'est un plaisir de souveraine.
De Brétigny has lost the game!	L'ami Guillot se ruinera.
He has brought all these dancers here.	Et son rival enragera.

BRETIGNY

| My friend Guillot must be insane | L'ami Guillot se ruinera |
| To have brought all these dancers here! | Avoir fait venir l'Opéra! |

GUILLOT
(aside, gleefully)

Now here are Venus and Adonis.	C'est un plaisir de souveraine,
And my victory is complete!	Avoir fait venir l'Opéra
I've brought them all to Cours-la-Reine!	Et son ballet au Cours-la-Reine,

(imitating the dancers' movements)

| Brétigny has lost the game! | Mon rival enragera! |
| He has lost the game! | Il enragera! |

Divertissement.

MANON
(to herself, aside, disturbed)

| No, his life and his heart are tied to mine forever! | Non, sa vie à la mienne est pour jamais liée, |
| He can't have forgotten me ... | Il ne peut m'avoir oubliée ... |

(seeing Lescaut nearby)

| Cousin, my chair! | Ma chaise, mon cousin. |

LESCAUT
(preparing to leave)

| Where do you want to go My dear? | Où faut-il vous porter Cousine? |

MANON

| To St Sulpice. | A Saint-Sulpice! |

LESCAUT

| What a strange idea! | Quel est ce bizarre caprice? |
| Did I hear you correctly? | Pardonnez-moi de faire répéter. |

MANON

| To St Sulpice. | A Saint-Sulpice! |

GUILLOT
(on one knee, to Manon)

| Venus of my life | Eh bien, maîtresse de ma vie, |
| How do you like the new ballet? | Qu'en dites-vous? |

MANON
(troubled)

| Ah, I haven't been watching! | Je n'ai rien vu! ... |

GUILLOT
(stunned)

| Haven't been watching? Is that my reward? | Rien vu? ... voilà le prix de ma galanterie! ... |
| Surely I deserve better! | Est-ce là ce qui m'était dû? |

The curtain falls to a reprise of the chorus. [16]

82

Second Tableau. The parlour of the seminary at Saint-Sulpice. The architecture is very simple 18th century. Between two pillars in the centre is a large door with a grille. There is oak panelling all around the parlour, up to about half way on the walls; benches, also of old oak, form part of the panelling. The upper section of the walls is painted with white lime. On either side of the door at the back hang two devotional pictures (the Lesueur type). A small door to the right, downstage. The great organ is heard before the curtain rises. [19]

Scene One. *Devout aristocratic and bourgeoise women are leaving the chapel of the seminary.*

FEMALE CHORUS
(to each other speaking of Des Grieux)

Ah, what a preacher!	Quelle éloquence,
Authority and grace!	L'admirable orateur!
A spiritual face!	Quelle abondance,
Ah, what a preacher!	Le grand prédicateur!
And what a sweet, silvery voice!	Et dans sa voix quelle douceur,
A silver voice and so inspiring!	Quelle douceur et quelle flamme!
Yes, hearing him, fervent joy	Comme en l'écoutant, la ferveur
Is flooding through my soul to the depths of my being!	Pénètre doucement jusqu'au fond de nos âmes!

How vividly too,	De quel art divin
He brought before us,	Il a, dans sa thèse,
The life of St Anne	Peint Saint Augustin
And St Theodorus!	Et Sainte Thérèse!
He too is a saint,	Lui-même est un saint!
An absolute saint!	C'est un fait certain,
He's a saint from heaven!	N'est-ce pas, ma chère?
Don't you think?	C'est un saint!
I am sure!	C'est certain!
He's a saint!	C'est un saint!

Enter Des Grieux. The devout women speak of him reverently to each other.

It's he! The Abbé Des Grieux!	C'est lui, c'est l'abbé Des Grieux,
You notice how he lowers his eyes.	Voyez comme il baisse les yeux!

Exeunt the devout and faithful, after having bowed to Des Grieux with deep curtseys.

Scene Two. *Des Grieux, Count Des Grieux.*

COUNT

Bravo, my boy, a great success.	Bravo, mon cher, succès complet,
Our family should be proud	Notre maison doit être fière
To have a new Bossuet among them!	D'avoir parmi les siens un nouveau Bossuet.

DES GRIEUX

Please father, spare me your irony.	De grâce, épargnez-moi, mon père!

Silence.

COUNT

So Chevalier, you are really proposing	Et, c'est pour de bon, Chevalier,
To devote the rest of your life to heaven for good and all.	Que tu prétends au ciel pour jamais te lier?

DES GRIEUX

I am, since life for me	Oui, je n'ai trouvé dans la vie
Has brought only bitterness and disgust.	Qu'amertume et dégoût ...

COUNT
(with gentle irony)

Those are strong words to use!	Les grands mots que voilà!
Has my son only learned to suffer?	Quelle route as-tu donc suivie?
This life has rich blessings to offer.	Et que sais-tu de cette vie
You are young and you must not refuse!	Pour penser qu'elle finit là?

Bring home to me a loving daughter, [20]	Epouse quelque brave fille,
Worthy to bear our ancient name;	Digne de nous, digne de toi,

*Geoffrey Chard as Count Des Grieux and John Brecknock as Des Grieux in the ENO 1982
production. (photo: Andrew March)*

Become a husband and a father,
And live in honour, not in shame:
Then Heaven will ask nothing further;
Just do what is right, do you hear?

When virtue needs to blow a trumpet,
It isn't virtue any more!

Deviens un père de famille
Ni pire, ni meilleur que moi.
Le ciel n'en veut pas davantage,
C'est là le devoir, entends-tu? ...

La vertu qui fait du tapage
N'est déjà plus de la vertu! ...

DES GRIEUX
(after a silence)

Nothing can prevent me
From taking my vows.

Rien ne peut m'empêcher
De prononcer mes voeux.

COUNT

Is that your last word?

C'est dit alors?

DES GRIEUX

It is!

Oui, je le veux!

COUNT

So be it.
I will pass through this door alone
... and tell my family
That we have a new saint among us ...
I can think of a few who won't believe me.

Soit!
Je franchirai donc seul cette grille
Et vais leur annoncer là-bas,
Qu'ils ont un saint dans la famille;
J'en sais beaucoup qui ne me croiront
pas! ...

DES GRIEUX

Don't make fun of me father, I beg you!

Ne raillez pas, monsieur, je vous en prie!

COUNT
(moved)

[One more word: —] As it's fairly certain

That you won't be presented with a benefice
Or an abbey overnight,
I shall be sending you
30,000 Louis.

Un mot encore: — Comme il n'est pas
certain
Que l'on te donne ici, du jour au lendemain,
Un bénéfice, une abbaye,
Je vais dès ce soir t'envoyer
Trente mille livres ...

DES GRIEUX

[My father ...]

Mon père ...

COUNT

It belongs to you — your share of your
mother's estate.
And now my son, farewell!

C'est à toi, c'est ta part sur le bien de ta
mère!
Et maintenant ... adieu, mon fils!

DES GRIEUX

God be with you father!

Adieu, mon père!

COUNT

And with you. Stay here and pray.

Adieu ... reste à prier!

Exit.

Scene Three. *Des Grieux, then the Porter.*

DES GRIEUX
(alone)

He has gone! I'm alone with God my
Saviour!
The only gift I pray for
Is holy peace of mind which my faith
brings me now.
Yes, I have tried to put my Saviour
Between the world and me!

Je suis seul! seul enfin! ... C'est le moment
suprême!
Il n'est plus rien que j'aime
Que le repos sacré que m'apporte la foi!

Oui, j'ai voulu mettre Dieu même
Entre le monde et moi!

Ah! Begone, dream of love, dream I lived [21]
for and cherished.
Do not cloud my repose, won after sore
distress;
I have drained sorrow's cup — every fair
hope has perished;
Ah, my heart ached and bled, I prayed for
sweet release!
Ah begone, begone, dream of love, long
begone.

There's no purpose in living or this
pretence of glory!
All I want is to drive forever from my
memory . . .
A cursed name, a name, an obsession. Ah,
but why?

Ah! fuyez, douce image à mon âme trop
chère,
Respectez un repos cruellement gagné,
Et songez, si j'ai bu dans une coupe amère
Que mon cœur l'emplirait de ce qu'il a
saigné!
Ah! fuyez! fuyez! loin de moi! Ah! fuyez!

Que m'importe la vie et ce semblant de
gloire!
Je ne veux que chasser du fond de ma
mémoire
Un nom maudit! . . . Ce nom qui m'obsède
. . . et pourquoi?

Distant sound of organ music can be heard.

PORTER

The service is beginning!

C'est l'office!

DES GRIEUX

I'll come now!

J'y vais!

DES GRIEUX
(to himself)

Dear God, have mercy upon me
And purify my spirit
Let your eternal light dispel
Shadows that linger still in the depths of
my heart!
Ah, begone dream of love I lived for and
cherished! . . .

Mon Dieu, de votre flamme
Purifiez mon âme,
Et dissipez à sa lueur
L'ombre qui passe encore dans le fond de
mon cœur!
Ah! fuyez, douce image, à mon âme trop
chère! . . .

(Exit.)

Scene Four. *The Porter.*

PORTER

He is young and his faith
Seems sincere . . . he made a great im-
pression
On the fair ladies
Of the congregation!

Il est jeune . . . et sa foi
Semble sincère . . . il a fait grand émoi
Parmi les plus belles
De nos fidèles!

Scene Five. *The Porter, Manon. Enter Manon.*

MANON
(tensely)

Monsieur, I want to speak to the Abbé Des
Grieux.

Monsieur . . . je veux parler . . . à l'abbé
Des Grieux!

PORTER

Certainly!

Fort bien!

MANON
(giving him money)

Here!

Tenez!

The Porter of the Seminary bows and goes out.

Scene Six. *Manon.*

MANON

These silent walls! . . .
This cold air I breathe . . .

Ces murs silencieux . . .
Cet air froid qu'on respire . . .

I hope this hasn't changed his feelings . . .	Pourvu que tout cela n'ait pas changé son cœur!
And left him without pity for a stupid mistake.	Devenu sans pitié pour une folle erreur,
I only hope his heart hasn't turned against me!	Pourvu qu'il n'ait pas appris à maudire!

The Magnificat is heard being sung in the chapel. She listens.

They are praying . . . Ah, how I should like to pray!	Là-bas . . . on prie . . . Ah! je voudrais prier! . . .
Pardon my sins, God, almighty creator!	Pardonnez-moi, Dieu de toute puissance,
If I dared to ask for your help,	Car si j'ose vous supplier
If I could hope you would forgive me,	En implorant votre clémence,
If my voice had the power to be heard in the skies . . .	Si ma voix de si bas peut monter jusqu'aux cieux,
Ah! I would beg for the heart of my dear Des Grieux!	C'est pour vous demander le cœur de Des Grieux.
Can you forgive my sins?	Pardonnez-moi, mon Dieu!

Scene Seven. *Manon, Des Grieux. Enter Des Grieux upstage.*

MANON
(in anguish)

Des Grieux!	C'est lui!

Manon turns away, ready to faint. Des Grieux comes forward.

DES GRIEUX
(almost spoken)

You! Here!	Toi! . . . vous!

MANON

Yes, I'm here Des Grieux! I am here.	Oui, c'est moi! moi! c'est moi!

DES GRIEUX

I do not want you here. Now go. Leave me alone.	Que viens-tu faire ici? . . . va-t'en! éloigne-toi . . .

MANON
(sorrowfully and pleadingly)

Yes, I caused you pain and you blame me!	Oui, je fus cruelle et coupable!
Will you not recall how we loved?	Mais rappelez-vous tant d'amour!
In those angry eyes that disdain me,	Ah! dans ce regard qui m'accable,
I read the memory of our love.	Lirai-je mon pardon un jour?

DES GRIEUX

Leave me alone.	Eloigne-toi!

MANON

Yes, I caused you pain and you blame me.	Oui, je fus cruelle et coupable!
Ah, you must remember our love!	Rappelez-vous tant d'amour!
Remember how once we loved.	Rappelez-vous tant d'amour!

DES GRIEUX

No, it was a dream, a delusion.	Non, j'avais écrit sur le sable
A vision of love past compare;	Ce rêve insensé d'un amour
How I revelled in my illusion,	Que le ciel n'avait fait durable

(bitterly)

Till I saw it fade into air.	Que pour un instant, pour un jour!

MANON

Ah, I see you blame me!	Oui! je fus coupable!
Yes, I caused you heartache!	Oui! Je fus cruelle!

DES GRIEUX

You betrayed me, Manon.	Ah! perfide Manon!

MANON
(approaching)

I'm ready to repent!   Si je me repentais . . .

DES GRIEUX

You betrayed me, betrayed me!   Ah! perfide! perfide!

MANON

And have you no pity   Est-ce que tu n'aurais
In your heart?   Pas de pitié?

DES GRIEUX
(interrupting her)

No, I could never trust you.   Je ne veux pas vous croire,
No, I will not remember you, I will not   Non, vous êtes sortie enfin de ma mémoire
    trust you . . .
I tore you from my heart!   Ainsi que de mon cœur!

MANON
(in tears)

Alas! The bird takes flight   Hélas! l'oiseau qui fuit
Away from happy bondage   Ce qu'il croit l'esclavage,
And then alone one night   Le plus souvent la nuit,
Comes flying in despair to batter at the   D'un vol désespéré revient battre au
    glass cage!   vitrage!
Forgive the wrong.   Pardonne-moi . . .

DES GRIEUX

No!   Non!

MANON

I beg you on my knees.   Je meurs à tes genoux!
(in a burst of despair)
Ah, return to your love . . . Do not try to   Ah! Rends-moi ton amour si tu veux que je
    deny it!   vive!

DES GRIEUX

No, it is dead to you!   Non! Il est mort pour vous!

MANON
(with spirit)

Is it really so dead that I cannot revive it?   L'est-il donc à ce point que rien ne le ravive!
    Listen to me!   Ecoute-moi!
    Don't you recall . . .   Rappelle-toi . . .
(with great charm, very affectionately)
Don't you feel my hand here on your hand [22] N'est-ce plus ma main que cette main
    pressing?   presse?
    Won't you turn and see?   N'est-ce plus ma voix?
Don't you know my touch tenderly   N'est-elle pour toi plus une caresse,
    caressing,
    As it used to be?   Tout comme autrefois?
And these eyes you loved, do they still   Et ces yeux, jadis pour toi pleins de
    disarm you?   charmes,
(with a sob)
Even through my tears won't they always   Ne brillent-ils plus à travers mes larmes?
    charm you?
(deeply moved, breathless)
Am I not the same? Am I not Manon?   Ne suis-je plus moi? n'ai-je plus mon nom?
Won't you look at me? Ah, look at me!   Ah! regarde-moi! Regarde-moi!
Don't you feel my hand tenderly caressing,   N'est-ce plus ma main que cette main
                                            presse?
    As it used to be?   Tout comme autrefois?
Won't you turn and see? Am I not Manon?   N'est-ce plus ma voix? . . . n'est-ce plus
                                            Manon?
    You recollect . . .   Rappelle-toi . . .
Don't you feel my hand?   N'est-ce plus ma main?

You can't forget! Won't you turn and see? Am I not the same? Am I not Manon? | Ecoute-moi: N'est-ce plus ma voix N'ai-je plus mon nom? N'est-ce plus Manon?

DES GRIEUX
(*in great confusion*)

Oh God, protect me now. I mustn't lose my courage. | O Dieu, soutenez-moi dans cet instant suprême!

MANON

I love you. I love you. | Je t'aime! Je t'aime!

DES GRIEUX
(*to Manon*)

Ah! No more. You must not talk of love in here . . . It is an outrage. Ah! No more. Don't talk to me of love. | Ah! Tais-toi! Ne parle pas d'amour ici, c'est un blasphème! Ah! Tais-toi! Ne parle pas d'amour!

MANON
(*feverishly*)

I love you. | Je t'aime!

Distant bell.

DES GRIEUX
(*listening with anguish*)

The service has begun! They are calling for me! | C'est l'heure de prier . . . on m'appelle là-bas . . .

MANON

No! You won't drive me away! | Non, je ne te quitte pas!

As Manon feverishly repeats her attempt to seduce him, Des Grieux is gradually more and more carried away.

DES GRIEUX
(*with spirit*)

Ah, Manon! My heart will have its way, I cannot tame it. | Ah, Manon! Je ne veux plus lutter, contre moi-même!

MANON
(*with a joyful cry*)

At last! | Enfin!

DES GRIEUX

Though my action bring down God's anger from the skies . . . My life is in your heart, my life is in your eyes! | Et, dusse-je sur moi faire crouler les cieux, Ma vie est dans ton cœur, ma vie est dans tes yeux!

(*exalted, with abandon*)

Ah! come Manon! I love you! | Ah! viens, Manon, je t'aime!

BOTH
(*ardently*)

I love you! | Je t'aime!

He falls into Manon's arms and runs off with her. Curtain.

Act Four

A large and luxurious room in the Hôtel de Transylvanie, separated from other rooms by broad alcoves. To the left, a window. Gaming tables have been set up in this and the other rooms. As the curtain rises, a crowd of gamblers surrounds the tables. [23]

Scene One. *Lescaut, Poussette, Javotte, Rosette, Croupiers, Gamblers, Card-sharpers.*

CROUPIERS
(*upstage*)

Place your bets, Messieurs!　　　　Faites vos jeux, messieurs!

GAMBLER

10,000 francs!　　　　　　　　Mille pistoles!

SECOND GAMBLER

I'll take you on!　　　　　　　　C'est tenu!

FIRST GAMBLER

Double the stakes!　　　　　　　Je double!

SECOND GAMBLER

Three aces!　　　　　　　　　　Brelan!

FIRST GAMBLER

I've lost!　　　　　　　　　　　C'est perdu!

TWO GAMBLERS
(*at the dice-table*)

Two! Five! Seven! Ten!　　　　　Deux! Cinq! Sept! Dix!

A VOICE
(*upstage*)

A hundred louis!　　　　　　　　Cent louis!

LESCAUT

Four hundred louis!　　　　　Quatre cent louis!
Hurrah! I have won!　　　　Vivat! . . . J'ai gagné.

A GAMBLER
(*pursuing Lescaut*)

I swear to you　　　　　　　　Je vous jure
This money belongs to me.　Que l'argent m'appartient!

LESCAUT

When somebody swears　　　Du moment qu'on l'assure
With as much confidence as you . . .　Avec autant d'aplomb . . .

GAMBLER

I had the ace and king.　　　　J'avais l'as et le roi!

LESCAUT

Let's play another hand then . . . It's all the　　Recommençons alors, çà m'est égal à moi!
same to me!

The Sharpers come cautiously forward.

SHARPERS
(*mezza voce, aside*)

If you gamble at random,　　　Le joueur sans prudence,
Chance will rule from the start;　Livre tout au hasard;
But to the man of wisdom,　　Mais le vrai sage pense
Playing cards is an art;　　　Que jouer est un art!

Luck is not to be trusted,	Pour la rendre opportune,
There's a much better way,	Nous savons sans danger
For we reckon the cards that we play	Quand il faut corriger
Can always be adjusted!	L'erreur de la fortune!

LESCAUT
(putting the money in his pocket)

I'm always honest when I play.	Tout en jouant honnêtement,
I fear I know no other way!	Je n'ai jamais fait autrement!

POUSSETTE, JAVOTTE AND ROSETTE
(They walk about, observing the Gamblers and the Sharpers; aside.)

In the rooms of the Transylvania	A l'hôtel de Transylvanie,
Gambling is the rage ... almost a mania;	Accourez tous, on vous en prie,
Once you begin ... gamble day and night ...	Passer vos jours et vos nuits,
Gold always comes to the fairest.	L'or vient tout seul aux plus belles,
And that is why we always win!	Et c'est nous qui gagnons toujours!

The Sharpers have done the rounds and return from the other side. Reprise of the Sharpers'
chorus. Lescaut returns triumphantly. He is surrounded by the Sharpers and by Poussette,
Javotte and Rosette.

LESCAUT
(heartily)

How I love her, how I adore her,	C'est ici que celle que j'aime
My angel, my sweet turtle dove!	A daigné fixer son séjour,
One day I will sing you a song	Et je vous dirai quelque jour
I have composed, specially for her,	Certains couplets que j'ai, moi-même,
Telling the story of our love!	Faits en l'honneur de notre amour!

(sound of gold, upstage)

Let that sweet sound, the chink of gold,	Et c'est ce bruit, ce bruit charmant,
Accompany what I unfold!	Qui leur sert d'accompagnement.

How I adore her, I have always been	Celle que j'aime ... je me pique
Close and discreet, I may say ...	D'être plein de discrétion ...
But still I will reveal her name ...	Pourtant, je vous dirai son nom ...

THE LADIES

Yes, her name.	Oui, son nom!

LESCAUT

Queen of Spades or Goddess of Fortune,	C'est Pallas, la dame de pique!
And there I end my sweet refrain!	Et là s'arrête ma chanson ...

(sound of gold upstage)

LESCAUT, SHARPERS AND THE LADIES

Let that sweet sound, the chink of gold,	Et c'est ce bruit, ce bruit charmant,
Accompany what { you / I } unfold!	Qui lui sert d'accompagnement!

Scene Two. *The same, Guillot. Guillot has just entered.*

GUILLOT
(to Lescaut)

Bravo, my friend!	Bravo, mon cher!

LESCAUT

Thank you!	Merci.

While Guillot is congratulating Lescaut, the Sharpers go back to the faro table. The Gamblers
have begun the game again, upstage, and Guillot has detained Lescaut and the three women.

GUILLOT
(with assurance)

I also am a poet	J'enfourche aussi Pégase,
From time to time; the Regent, there's a	De temps en temps! Ainsi, moi, j'ai sur le
pretty theme	régent

For a mischievous rhyme. I say nothing
    extreme ...
        You know it.
    My secret is cloaked in a veil ...
    But you will see the meaning of my tale.

Fait des vers très malins! Mais en homme
    prudent
        Je gaze!
Et passe les mots dangereux,
Vous allez voir, on ne comprend que
    mieux.

(cautiously)

When the ...
    Quand le ...

(he pantomimes what he is going to say)

    This is the Regent!
        Goes to see ...

    C'est le régent!
        Va voir ...

(same business)

      That's his mistress!
He says ...

      C'est sa maîtresse!
Il dit ...

(slyly)

    You understand?
And she replies ...
    Your Royal Highness! Tra la la!

    On me comprend?
Elle répond ...
    De Votre Altesse! Tra la la!

(to those who surround him)

Ah, it's so droll, so refined!
Ah! C'est badin, c'est léger ...

LESCAUT AND THE LADIES
(laughing)

And who could say you'd been unkind?
Et l'on ne court aucun danger!

GUILLOT

Ah, it's so sharp! It's so droll and refined!
C'est piquant! C'est badin! C'est léger!

GUILLOT, LESCAUT AND THE LADIES

Ssh ...
Chut ...

    Great uproar. Everyone gets up to look at the people who are coming in.

Scene Three. *The same. Enter Manon and Des Grieux.*

GUILLOT

But who is everyone making such a fuss of?
Mais qui donc nous arrive et fait tout ce
    tapage? ...

POUSSETTE, JAVOTTE AND ROSETTE

It's the lovely Manon! With her young
    chevalier!

C'est la belle Manon avec son chevalier.

They move away.

DES GRIEUX
(looking sadly and apprehensively about)

So here I am. I should not have agreed,
    But I found I hadn't the courage.

M'y voici donc! j'aurais dû résister!
Je n'en ai pas eu le courage.

GUILLOT
(vexed)

Des Grieux!
Le chevalier ...

LESCAUT
(to Guillot)

    What a face!
They appear to annoy you!

    Vous changez de visage,
Et quelque chose ici, paraît vous irriter ...

GUILLOT

I have every right to be annoyed ...
I adored Manon and I feel upset
    And wounded
That she should prefer another man to me!

A bon droit je fais la grimace,
Car j'adorais Manon et je trouve blessant
    Et froissant
Qu'elle en aime un autre à ma place!

Lescaut leads Guillot away.

Place your bets, Messieurs!	Faites vos jeux, Messieurs!

All return to the game. Manon and Des Grieux have remained alone, downstage. Manon, seeing that Des Grieux is still sad, comes closer to him.

MANON

In your heart, Des Grieux, will I always be ruler?	De ton cœur, Des Grieux, suis-je plus souveraine?

DES GRIEUX
(with passionate impetuosity)

Manon, sphinx I adore, you have charmed me forever! Heart of woman supreme! . . . How I love you and hate you! Pleasure and gold are all you seem to long for. Ah! You are are quite insane, But I adore you.	[24] Manon, sphinx étonnant, véritable sirène! . . . Cœur trois fois féminin . . . que je t'aime et te hais! Pour le plaisir et l'or quelle ardeur inouîe! Ah! folle que tu es! Comme je t'aime!

MANON
(with perfidious voluptuousness)

And I . . . I'd love you evermore If you'd agree!	Et moi, comme je t'aimerais! Si tu voulais . . .

DES GRIEUX

If I'd agree?	Si je voulais?

MANON
(changing her tone, coming back to reality)

Our life of pleasure now is over . . . Chevalier, all our money gone! But in here, when you need to win . . . A pile of gold is easy to recover!	Notre opulence est envolée, Chevalier, nous n'avons plus rien! Mais ici, quand on le veut bien, Une fortune est vite retrouvée . . .

DES GRIEUX
(disturbed)

Ah, don't say that, Manon!	Que me dis-tu, Manon?

LESCAUT
(drawing closer to Manon)

Manon is right, In faro all you need is luck. A pile of gold is easy to recover!	Elle a raison! En quelques coups de pharaon, Une fortune est vite retrouvée . . .

DES GRIEUX
(disturbed)

What me? Play cards! I can't! I won't!	Qui? moi? jouer? . . . jamais! jamais!

LESCAUT

Now you are wrong! Manon cannot live without money . . .	Vous avez tort! Manon n'aime pas la misère.

MANON

Chevalier, if you really love me, Say yes, and very soon you'll see We'll win a fortune!	Chevalier, si je te suis chère, Consens, et tu verras qu'après, Nous serons riches . . .

LESCAUT

Very likely! Fortune's Goddess is only fickle hearted With gamblers who know how to play And who offer her battle each day.	C'est probable! La fortune n'est intraitable Qu'avec le joueur éprouvé Qui contre elle souvent a lutté.

| But when she sees a novice she is gentle and tender! | Elle est douce, au contraire, à celui qui commence! |

MANON
(to Des Grieux)

| Des Grieux say you will! | Tu veux bien, n'est-ce-pas? |

DES GRIEUX

| I am mad to consider! | Infernale démence! |

LESCAUT
(hurrying him)

| Come on! | Venez! |

DES GRIEUX
(to Manon)

| I've given you my soul! What can you offer me? | Je t'aurai tout donné! mais qu'aurai-je en retour? |

LESCAUT
(hurrying him)

| You're sure to win! | Vous gagnerez! |

MANON
(with spirit)

| My body and my soul, my life and all my love! | Mon être tout entier, ma vie et mon amour! |

DES GRIEUX
(with passionate impetuosity)

| Manon, sphinx I adore, you have charmed me forever! | Manon, sphinx étonnant, véritable sirène! |

LESCAUT

You are certain of winning!	Votre chance est certaine,
You have to play and play forever!	Jouez toujours! jouez sans cesse!
You have to play, it's such a joy!	Jouez toujours, c'est le bonheur!
Play on and play again! Come on!	Jouez, jouez encore! Venez!

DES GRIEUX

Heart of women supreme!	Cœur trois fois féminin!
How I love you and hate you!	Que je t'aime et te hais!
Pleasure and gold are all you seem to long for!	Pour le plaisir et l'or quelle ardeur inouïe!
Ah, you are quite insane and I adore you!	Ah! folle que tu es! comme je t'aime!
Ah, must it be that, out of weakness . . .	Ah! faut-il donc que ma faiblesse,
I sacrifice my honour too! All that I hold most dear!	Te donne jusqu'à mon honneur?

MANON

You must rely on my devotion!	Repose-toi sur ma tendresse,
And never doubt my loving heart.	Ne doute jamais de mon cœur!
Ah, our happiness is now! You cannot ever doubt!	Ah! c'est là notre bonheur!
My love is for you, for you my whole being!	A toi mon amour! A toi tout mon être!

Guillot enters with Javotte and Poussette.

GUILLOT
(to Des Grieux)

One word if you please chevalier:	Un mot s'il vous plaît, chevalier!
I've a proposal — a game of faro . . .	Je vous propose une partie.
Then we shall see if you're lucky at cards	Nous verrons si sur moi vous devez l'emporter
As well as love . . .	Toujours . . .

JAVOTTE
(gaily)

Bravo Guillot, I'll take a bet on you.   Bravo, Guillot, pour vous, moi, je parie . . .

POUSSETTE
(gaily)

I'll take you on; my bet is on the   Et je parie alors, moi, pour ce
Chevalier.   chevalier . . .

GUILLOT
(to Des Grieux)

Do you accept?   Acceptez-vous?

DES GRIEUX
(disturbed)

I accept!   J'accepte . . .

The Croupiers can be heard in the background saying 'Faites vos jeux, messieurs.'

GUILLOT

Chevalier.   Commençons.

POUSSETTE

Our bet is still the same?   Nous parions toujours!

JAVOTTE AND ROSETTE

Yes, still the same.   Nous parions!

GUILLOT

Ten thousand francs!   Mille pistoles!

DES GRIEUX

Right, Monsieur! Ten thousand francs.   Soit, monsieur, mille pistoles . . .

LESCAUT
(with rapturous admiration)

Ten thousand francs! I'll try my luck, here   Mille pistoles! A moi, Pallas, à moi!
goes.

He goes off to gamble at another table.

MANON

All this wild excitement . . .   Ces ivresses folles . . .
Ah! This is living! It's the way I want to live!   C'est la vie, ou du moins c'est celle que je
                                                              veux!

THE LADIES

This is living!   C'est la vie!

THE DEALERS
(upstage)

Place your bets Messieurs!   Faites vos jeux, Messieurs!

MANON
(taking the glass which Javotte has given her)

Glitter of gold and laughter, these sudden   Ce bruit de l'or, ce rire et ces éclats joyeux!
cries of joy!
A lifetime of love and roses!   A nous les amours et les roses!
Singing, loving, sweetly enclose us . . .   Chanter, aimer, sont douces choses,
We pass every minute in play!   Qui sait si nous vivrons demain!
Who thinks of tomorrow today?   Qui sait si nous vivrons demain!

The ladies repeat this refrain.

Youth and beauty wither,   La jeunesse passe.
Fade away forever . . .   La beauté s'efface,
Let us only wish   Que tous nos désirs
For a life of bliss!   Soient pour les plaisirs!
Passionate embraces,   L'amour et les fièvres,

Happy, loving faces,	Sur toutes les lèvres
And Manon must have more	Pour Manon encore
Gold, still more and more!	De l'or, de l'or! . . .

GAMBLERS AND SHARPERS
(to Lescaut)

Come on.	Au jeu!

LESCAUT
(defending himself)

Permit me, if you please, to play on credit!	Permettez-moi de jouer sur parole!
I always keep my word!	Je suis de bonne foi!

GAMBLERS AND SHARPERS

The game!	Au jeu!

LESCAUT

I've nothing left! No gold, not even silver.	Plus un louis, pas même une pistole!
Not one. They took the lot. I'm done!	Plus rien! ils m'ont volé, moi . . . moi! . . .

GUILLOT
(to Des Grieux, while playing)

Your luck is really quite amazing.	Vous avez une chance folle!
Stake twenty thousand more!	Mille louis de plus!

DES GRIEUX
(feverishly)

	Right, Monsieur!	Soit, monsieur.
Double the stake!	Mille louis!	

GUILLOT

I have lost!	J'ai perdu!

MANON
(approaching the gamblers, to Des Grieux)

And so, did you win?	Eh bien! gagnes-tu?

DES GRIEUX
(showing her the gold and money bills)

You see it!	Regarde . . .

MANON

Is it ours?	C'est à nous?

DES GRIEUX

It is ours!	C'est à nous.

MANON

I adore you!	Je t'adore!

GUILLOT

I double! You agree?	Le double, voulez-vous?

DES GRIEUX

Agreed!	C'est dit!

GUILLOT

I'm still the loser!	Je perds encore!

MANON

I'm glad I made you play. I told you you would win!	Je te l'avais bien dit que tu devais gagner.

DES GRIEUX
(rapturously)

Manon! I love you! I love you!	Manon! Je t'aime! je t'aime!

GUILLOT
(leaving the table)

This game cannot continue!   J'arrête la partie!

DES GRIEUX
(getting up also)

If that is what you wish . . .   C'est comme vous voudrez.

GUILLOT
(maliciously)

You have imposed upon me . . .   Ce serait duperie
I see it all.   De s'obstiner.

DES GRIEUX
(changing his tone of voice, threatening)

Monsieur?   Plaît-il?

GUILLOT

That's enough! Understood.   Il suffit, je m'entends;
(with insolent irony)
You really are a skilful man!   Vous avez vraiment des talents!

DES GRIEUX
(angrily)

What did you say?   Que dites-vous?

GUILLOT

Ah, now he threatens!   Quelle furie!
Before he breaks his victim's head   Vouloir encore battre les gens
He likes to cheat him first!   Quand on les a volés!

DES GRIEUX
(springing at Guillot)

Dishonourable slander! You're a liar!   Infâme calomnie! . . . Misérable!

All come rushing in.

ALL

Messieurs, take care, take care, Messieurs!   Messieurs, voyons, voyons, messieurs,
Society is rigid, you must obey its laws!   Quand on est dans le monde il faut se tenir
                                         mieux!

GUILLOT
(very upset)

You witnessed it all Messieurs . . . My dear   Je prends à témoin, messieurs,
    young ladies!   mesdemoiselles . . .
(to Des Grieux and Manon)
As for you, you will hear from me, and very   Pour vous deux, vous aurez bientôt de mes
    shortly!   nouvelles!

Exit.

Scene Four. *The same less Guillot.*

CHORUS

Well such a thing has never happened!   La chose ne s'est jamais vue,
No, no, not here, no, never here!   Non, non jamais, certainement!
He wouldn't cheat us here in such a way!   On n'a volé jamais, pareillement.
(pointing at Des Grieux)
Is he the cheat? The cheat?   On a volé! c'est lui!

LESCAUT
(interposing)

Come on, Messieurs! Calm yourselves!   Voyons, messieurs! Calmez-vous!
(to Des Grieux)
Oh, what a bore? What have you done?   Ah! quel ennui! Qu'avez-vous fait?

The clumsy fool! Oh what a bore!   Le maladroit! Ah, quel ennui!

In the background, the croupiers repeat 'Now place your bets messieurs!'

MANON
(to Des Grieux)

Let's go! Oh, I implore you!   Partons, je t'en supplie,
Let's go quickly.   Partons vite . . .

DES GRIEUX
(firmly)

No, on my honour . . .   Non, sur ma vie!
If I go now perhaps they would believe   Si je partais, peut-être croirait-on
Guillot was right in slandering my name.   Qu'en m'accusant cet homme avait raison!

Loud knocking is heard at the door.

THE LADIES, LESCAUT AND SHARPERS
(aside)

Who's that? Who's making all that clatter?   Eh! mais, qui frappe de la sorte?

Renewed knocking is heard.

GAMBLERS

Hide all the gold!   Vite, vite, cachez l'argent!

MANON
(aside, puzzled)

Who's knocking? What's the matter?   Qui frappe à cette porte?
I'm frightened yet I don't know why.   Je tremble, je ne sais pourquoi!

A VOICE
(offstage)

Open in the name of the King!   Ouvrez! au nom du roi!

LESCAUT

The police!   Un exempt de police!
Come let's get out of here.   Gagnons vite le toit!

Lescaut escapes.

Scene Five. *The same without Lescaut. Guillot, the Count, Police Officer followed by guardsmen.*

GUILLOT
(pointing out Des Grieux)

This is the guilty man . . .   Le coupable est monsieur . . .
(pointing out Manon)
and that is his accomplice.   et voilà sa complice.

MANON
(to Guillot under her breath)

You disgust me!   Misérable!

GUILLOT
(to Manon)

A thousand regrets   Mille regrets,
Mademoiselle,   Mademoiselle,
But the chance was too good to miss.   Mais la partie était trop belle.
(in a whisper)
I told you I would be revenged!   Je vous avais bien dit que je me vengerais.
(to Des Grieux)
I've had my revenge on you too, young   J'ai pris ma revanche, mon maître!
master!
No doubt you will manage to console   Il faudra vous en consoler.
yourself.

DES GRIEUX
(violently)

I'll do my best! And I think I'll begin
  By throwing you out of the window!

J'y tâcherai! Mais je vais commencer
  Par vous jeter par la fenêtre!

GUILLOT
(scornfully)

Out of the window!

Par la fenêtre! ...

COUNT
(to the Chevalier, calmly)

And I? Will I be thrown out too?

Et moi! ... M'y jetez-vous aussi?

DES GRIEUX

My father, in this place?
You?

Mon père! ... vous ici! ...
Vous!

MANON

His father!

Son père! ...

COUNT

Can I still set you free from dishonour,
  And save you from this life of shame?
Are you mad? Don't you see your discredit
  Will soon threaten me and my name?

Oui, je viens t'arracher à la honte
  Qui chaque jour grandit sur toi,
Insensé, vois-tu pas qu'elle monte
  Et va s'élever jusqu'à moi!

Can I still rescue you from dishonour?
  No, in spite of your look which implores me,
I won't relent! No: I won't relent!
  The honour of our name comes first!

Oui, je viens t'arracher à la honte!
  Et malgré ton regard qui m'implore,
Pas de pardon! Non, pas de pardon!
  Je dois veiller sur notre honneur!

DES GRIEUX
(to his father, with great feeling)

Ah, you see how I beg and implore you!
  Do not now be harsh and severe,
My remorse will gnaw at my heart evermore!
  I beg you, won't you save my name?

Ah! comprends ce regard qui t'implore,
  Qui voudrait fléchir ta rigeur!
Le remords, tu le vois, me dévore, à jamais!
  Ne peux-tu sauver mon honneur?

MANON
(with great feeling, in despair)

Ah, I see now the future will part us!
  And my heart is trembling with fear!
Cruel torment will gnaw at my heart evermore!
  Is all my happiness now gone?

O douleur, l'avenir nous sépare!
  Et d'effroi mon cœur est tremblant!
Un tourment trop cruel me dévore à jamais!

  Est-ce donc fait de mon bonheur?

GUILLOT

So I take my revenge!
  What a sudden and terrible vengeance!
No, I won't relent!
  The law will now take care of you!

Me voilà donc vengé!
  Ma vengeance est terrible, elle est prompte.
Non! pas de pitié!
  Vous appartenez à la loi!

THE LADIES, GAMBLERS AND SHARPERS

Ah, give in to her tears!
She is so lovely!
Mercy! Your heart must feel
Some pity for so fair a child!

Ah! cédez à ses pleurs!
Pour sa jeunesse!
Grâce! Tant de beauté
Mérite que l'on ait pitié!

COUNT
(pointing to Des Grieux)

Off to prison!

Qu'on l'emmène!

(aside, to Des Grieux)

And later you will be set free.

Plus tard on vous délivera.

DES GRIEUX
(with anxiety, indicating Manon)

And Manon?   Mais elle?

GUILLOT
(interrupting)

She'll go where she deserves . . .   Le guet la conduira
She'll be transported as a convict.   Où l'on emmène ses pareilles!

DES GRIEUX
(with spirit)

Don't move a step!   N'approchez-pas,
(throwing himself in front of Manon)
Now I swear to defend her.   Je saurai la défendre!

MANON
(fainting)

Ah, all is lost. I'll die! Mercy!   Ah! c'en est fait! . . . je meurs. Grâce!
(with a supreme effort)
Ah, I'll die!   Ah! pitié!

DES GRIEUX
(in despair)

Ah Manon! They will part us forever!   O douleur! l'avenir nous sépare à jamais!

THE LADIES, GAMBLERS AND SHARPERS

Ah, forgive!   Ah! pitié!

COUNT AND GUILLOT

No, no more!   Non, jamais!

Curtain.

Des Grieux (John Brecknock) protests at Guillot's insinuations, ENO, 1978 (photo: Andrew March)

Act Five

The road to Le Havre. A dusty track. Some trees dried up by the sea wind; gorse and broom grow on a bank on the right; at the back a sunken road; the sea is on the horizon. It is the end of the day. [25]

Scene One. *Des Grieux.*

DES GRIEUX
(seated alone)

Manon! Wretched Manon!	Manon! pauvre Manon!
I can see you in chains with all those other women!	Je te vois enchaînée avec ces misérables,
And in some filthy tumbril. Oh God have you no pity?	Et la charrette passe! . . . O cieux inexorables,
I'm driven to despair!	Faut-il désespérer?

Scene Two. *Des Grieux, Lescaut.*

DES GRIEUX
(seeing Lescaut)

No! Lescaut!	Non! C'est lui! . . .

(going to him, feverishly)

Your escort is all ready!	Prépare ton escorte!
Look the guards are over there . . . they are coming this way.	Les archers sont là-bas . . . ils arrivent ici . . .
Your men know what to do? Let them stay true and steady	Tes hommes sont armés? . . . Ils nous prêtent main forte
And we will set her free.	Et nous la délivrons! . . .

(seeing that Lescaut has not replied)

Well, isn't that the plan?	Quoi? . . . N'est-ce pas ainsi
You've got it all arranged! Come on, why don't you answer?	Que tout est convenu? . . . Tu gardes le silence?

LESCAUT
(ashamedly, with effort)

My poor innocent friend . . .	Monsieur le chevalier . . .

DES GRIEUX
(anxiously)

Lescaut?	Eh bien?

LESCAUT

I'm sorry,	Je pense
Everything is lost.	Que tout est perdu!

DES GRIEUX

What?	Quoi?

LESCAUT

As soon as they saw the guns	Dès qu'au soleil ont lui
Of the royal patrol all the cowards ran off.	Les mousquets des archers, tous ces lâches ont fui! . . .

DES GRIEUX
(distraught)

You lie! For God has taken pity on my anguish!	Tu mens! . . . Le ciel a pris pitié de ma souffrance!
In an hour she'll be safely rescued . . .	C'est l'instant de la délivrance,
I shall comfort Manon once again in my arms!	Tout à l'heure Manon va tomber dans mes bras!

LESCAUT
(sadly)

What I have said is true!	Je ne vous trompe pas!

DES GRIEUX
(making a gesture as if to strike him)

Oh God!   Va-t'en!

LESCAUT
(kneeling before him)

Now look! What can I do? I serve the king . . .   Frappez! Que voulez-vous? . . . On est
                                                       soldat, le roi
A soldier's pay is poor! And so against my   Paie assez mal . . . Alors, bien malgré soi,
will,
(in tears)
I lose my honest name and then you all   On devient un coquin, un homme abomin-
despise me!   able!

DES GRIEUX
(roughly)

Oh God!   Va-t'en!

They hear a noise offstage. They listen speechless.

GUARDS
(offstage)

Little captain, say,   Capitaine, ô gué,
Do you like the way   Es-tu fatigué
We have marched all day?   De nous voir à pied!

Ah, no! Captain charming,   Mais non! La Ramée,
As you ride your horse,   On n'est pas trop mal
You have no remorse   Sur un bon cheval,
For the poor old army!   Pour mener l'armée.

DES GRIEUX
(listening)

What is that?   Qu'est cela?

LESCAUT

They are here, I'm certain . . .   Ce sont eux, sans doute!
(going along the road)
I see them on the pathway!   Je les voie sur la route!

DES GRIEUX
(wishing to rush out impetuously)

Manon! Manon!   Manon! Manon!
(Lescaut stops him.)
I only have my sword!   Je n'ai que mon épée,
I have no choice, we must attack the troop.   Mais nous allons les attaquer tous deux!

LESCAUT
(exclaiming)

What a crazy idea!   Quelle folle équipée!

DES GRIEUX

Come on!   Allons!

LESCAUT

There's not a chance! Des Grieux,   Vous la perdrez! . . . Croyez-moi,
We will have to find some other way.   Il vaut mieux prendre un autre moyen . . .

DES GRIEUX

But what?   Lequel?

LESCAUT

You must be patient!   Je vous en prie!
This way!   Partons!

DES GRIEUX
(resisting)

No, no!   Non, non!

LESCAUT

You'll see Manon, I give my word!   Vous la verrez, je le promets!

DES GRIEUX

But leave! When I can   Partir! lorsque
Hear her call me: Son cœur me crie:
'Des Grieux'! — No, I won't!   'Viens á moi!' — Non, jamais!

LESCAUT

Now if you love Manon!   Si vous l'aimez, venez!

DES GRIEUX

Ah, if I love her . . .   Ah! Si je l'aime!
When I would gladly risk my life,   Quand je veux tout braver,
When I would gladly die to save her!   Quand je voudrais mourir pour elle!

LESCAUT

Then come!   Venez!

DES GRIEUX

When shall I see her?   Quand la verrai-je?

LESCAUT

In just a moment!   A l'instant même!

He draws Des Grieux behind the bushes.

Scene Three. *The same, hidden. Guards. A Sergeant. The Guards are now close behind and constantly coming nearer.*

GUARDS

Little captain, say,   Capitaine, ô gué!
Do you like the way   Es-tu fatigué,
We have marched all day?   De nous voir à pied,

Ah, no! Captain charming,   Mais non, La Ramée,
As you ride your horse,   On n'est pas trop mal
You have no remorse   Sur un bon cheval
For the poor old army.   Pour mener l'armée.

Little captain, say,   Capitaine, ô gué,
Have we come half-way   Est-ce que je boirai,
    Today?   Au gué,
Have we come half-way?   Capitaine, ô gué!

The Guards appear on stage.

ONE OF THE GUARDS
(to the Sergeant)

All right, give them a rest.   Après chanter, il faut boire!

SERGEANT

It isn't a very heroic task for a soldier, it it, C'est bien le moins! . . . car ce n'est pas la gloire,

Escorting ladies of easy virtue   D'escorter l'arme au bras et de faire embarquer

Into exile.   Des demoiselles sans vertu!

GUARDS

What a life   C'est se moquer
For a soldier!   De nous!

SERGEANT

Never mind.   N'importe!

103

It's our job. And what do the charming prisoners
Say about it?

C'est le métier! . . . Et que disent là-bas
Les captives?

GUARDS

Not a murmur out of them.
One of them's very sick, I think she's dying!

Oh! rien! . . . Elles ne bougent pas!
L'une d'elles est déjà malade, à demi morte.

SERGEANT

Which one is that?

Laquelle?

GUARD

The one who hides
Her face and weeps if you try
To talk to her.

Eh! celle qui cachait
Son visage, et pleurait quand l'un de nous cherchait
A lui parler.

SERGEANT

Manon you mean?

Manon, alors? . . .

DES GRIEUX
(behind the bushes)

Oh God!

O ciel!

LESCAUT
(holding him back)

Quiet!
Have you any money?

Silence!
Laissez-moi faire . . .

Des Grieux gives his purse to Lescaut and remains at a distance. Lescaut advances towards the Sergeant.

LESCAUT
(to the Sergeant, at a distance)

Hallo there comrade!

Hé, camarade!

SERGEANT

It's a soldier!

Un soldat! . . .

LESCAUT

Better still I hope —
A friend!

Mieux, je pense,
Un ami! . . .

(aside, to Des Grieux)

[Have you any money?]

Avez-vous de l'argent?

(to the Sergeant)

You're an obliging fellow
I'm sure. I want to ask you a favour.

Vous êtes obligeant,
J'en suis sûr! . . . Je viens donc réclamer un service . . .

SERGEANT

A favour?

Et lequel?

LESCAUT

I'd just like to talk for a few minutes
To . . . the poor girl who's so sick.

C'est rien que pour un instant
De me laissez causer avec la pauvre fille
Dont vous parliez . . .

SERGEANT

Why?

Pourquoi?

LESCAUT

She's a relation of mine.

Je suis de sa famille . . .

SERGEANT

No, I can't help you!

Impossible!

104

LESCAUT

Ah!   Ah!

Lescaut gives him some money.

SERGEANT
(looking round to see if anyone saw him take it)

Still ...   Pourtant ...

LESCAUT
(giving him more money)

May I insist?   En insistant?

SERGEANT

Well, perhaps ...   Peut-être!

LESCAUT
(giving him still more money)

Then I do insist.   On insiste!

SERGEANT

Now you talk just like my master ...   Ah! ma foi, si vous parlez en maître!
So of course I obey!   Accordé! ...

(in a loud voice)

I am not as tough   Je ne suis pas si noir
As I look. The village is down there;   Que j'en ai l'air! ... Là-bas est le village,
You bring her back yourself this evening.   Vous l'y ramènerez vous-même, avant ce
                                             soir!

(to the guards)

Untie her.   Détachez-la!

LESCAUT

Thank you, my dear friend, and a pleasant   Merci, mon cher, et bon voyage!
journey to you.

SERGEANT

Now don't go and spoil it all   N'allez pas, pour me remercier,
By trying to carry her off!   Essayer de nous l'enlever!

LESCAUT
(raising his hand)

My word of honour!   J'en fais mon grand serment.
Need I say more!   En faut-il davantage?

SERGEANT

No, because one of my men will stay behind   Non, d'ailleurs quelqu'un restera,
To keep an eye on you.   Qui de loin vous surveillera!

LESCAUT

Dear friend I thank you from my heart!   Merci, mon cher, et bon voyage!

SERGEANT

Forward march!   En marche, allons!

DES GRIEUX
(hidden)

Merciful God, I thank you.   Merci, Dieu de bonté!

*The guards march off and their song gradually fades away in the distance. Des Grieux and
Lescaut look anxiously after them.*

CHORUS

Little captain, say   Capitaine, ô gué,
Do you like the way   Es-tu fatigué,
We have marched all day?   Pour mener l'armée ...

Scene Four. *Des Grieux, Lescaut.*

DES GRIEUX
(still hidden, to Lescaut, in a burst of feeling)

Manon! I am going to see her!   Manon! je vais la voir!

LESCAUT

And soon, I hope.   Et bientôt, je l'espère,
You could carry her off!   Vous pourrez l'emmener!

DES GRIEUX
(pointing to the guard left there by the sergeant)

But this soldier?   Ce soldat?

LESCAUT
(jingling the money left in the purse)

That's my business!   J'en fais mon affaire!
I did the right thing not to give it all away.   J'ai très bien fait de ne pas tout donner.

Lescaut goes back upstage. He talks with the guard for a moment and then leads him away. The soldiers' song can no longer be heard.

Scene Five. *Des Grieux, Manon. She enters painfully and as if broken by fatigue. She slowly comes down the little path. On seeing Des Grieux she utters a cry of joy.*

MANON

Ah! Des Grieux!   Ah! Des Grieux!

DES GRIEUX
(with wild delight, then almost spoken, with deep emotion)

O Manon! Manon! Manon!   O Manon! Manon! Manon!

Silence. Suddenly, Manon frees herself from Des Grieux's arms, falls to the ground and begins to weep bitterly. [26]

DES GRIEUX

You're weeping.   Tu pleures!

MANON
(her head in her hands, weeping)

Yes! In shame at myself, and in sorrow for you.   Oui, de honte sur moi, mais de douleur sur toi!

DES GRIEUX
(tenderly)

Manon! Look at me dearest, and think of the future!
We'll be happy again!   Manon ... lève la tête et ne songe qu'aux heures
D'un bonheur qui revient!

MANON
(bitterly)

Ah, it cannot   Ah! pourquoi
Be true.   Me tromper?

DES GRIEUX

Yes, the sentence they gave you.   Non, ces terres lointaines
Exile across the sea — comes to an ending here.   Dont ils te menaçaient, tu ne les verras pas!
You and I will escape ... And I promise to save you   Nous fuirons tous les deux! ... Au delà de ces plaines
From misery and fear!   Nous porterons nos pas! ...
(Manon is silent; affectionately)
Manon, you do not speak.   Manon! ... réponds-moi donc! ...

MANON
(with infinite tenderness)

I shall love you forever.   Seul amour de mon âme,

What a good man you are ... ah, so generous and free!	Je ne sais qu'aujourd'hui la bonté de ton cœur
I have fallen so low, alas, how can you ever	Et, si bas qu'elle soit, hélas! Manon réclame
Forgive or have pity on me!	Pardon, pitié pour son erreur!

(Des Grieux wishes to interrupt her.)

Let me! I beg! My heart was so fickle and faithless.	Non! ... non! ... encore! ... Mon cœur fût léger et volage
And even though I loved you	Et même en vous aimant
More than life,	Eperdument
Still I destroyed you!	J'étais ingrate! ...

DES GRIEUX

No Manon, you are blameless!	Ah! Pourquoi ce langage?

MANON
(continuing)

Just what I never can explain	Et je ne puis m'imaginer
Is how ... by what ignorant madness ...	Comment, et par quelle folie
I could cause you such pain,	J'ai pu vous chagriner
Or a moment of sadness!	Un seul jour de ma vie!

DES GRIEUX
(in a burst of feeling)

No more!	Assez! ...

MANON
(weeping)

I could tear out my heart	Je me hais et maudis en pensant
When I think of our beautiful love ... and the way we enjoyed it;	A ces douces amours, par ma faute brisées,
You lived your life for me alone ... and I for you.	Et je ne paierais pas assez de tout mon sang
Ah, how sweetly we loved! To think that I destroyed it!	La moitié des douleurs que je vous ai causées!
Forgive the wrong!	Pardonnez-moi!

(as if choked with sobs)

DES GRIEUX
(passionately moved)

What have I to forgive?	Qu'ai-je à te pardonner

(with spirit)

Now that you have come back, we must begin to live!	Quand ton cœur à mon cœur vient de se redonner!

MANON
(crying out with joy; transfigured)

Ah! I feel a glorious light Sent from heaven above	[27] Ah! Je sens une pure flamme M'éclairer de ses feux.

(increasingly moved)

Into my heart to light our love.	Je vois enfin les jours heureux!

DES GRIEUX
(rapturously)

O Manon, O my love, my wife,	O Manon! mon amour, ma femme,
You can see happy rays	Oui, ce jour radieux
Which unite all our days.	Nous unit tous les deux!
Our happy, happy days!	Voici les jours heureux!
Now God himself grants you	Oui, le ciel lui-même
Forgiveness. I love you!	Te pardonne ... Je t'aime!

MANON
(sensitively)

Then I can die in peace!	Ah! je puis donc mourir!

DES GRIEUX

Manon! No! Live!	Mourir! ... non, vivre! ...

Nothing to fear, as we go hand in hand | Et, sans dangers, désormais pouvoir suivre

Along our secret pathway, where joy will never cease! | Deux à deux ce chemin où tout va refleurir! ...

MANON
(as if in a dream)

Yes, maybe I can still be happy! | Oui ... je puis encore être heureuse!

(deeply moved, almost in a whisper)

Let's talk again about the past ... | Nous reparlerons du passé ...

(brokenly; slowly and tenderly)

The inn ... the coach ... and the leafy road. | De l'auberge ... du coche ... et de la route ombreuse

(with somewhat greater agitation)

The letter you wrote to your father ... | Du billet, par ta main tracé ...

(deeply moved)

Our little table ... and when I saw you | De la petite table ... et de ta robe noire

(gravely; with a sad smile)

At St Sulpice ... I remember each detail ... | A Sainte-Sulpice! ... Oh! j'ai bonne mémoire ...

DES GRIEUX

You are dreaming, Manon! | C'est un rêve charmant!

(joyfully)

All is ready; let us be on our way! | Tout s'apprête pour notre liberté!

MANON
(joyfully)

We'll go! | Partons!

(gradually growing weaker)

No! I cannot go further ... | Non, il m'est impossible ...

Cannot move ... any further ... My longing for sleep | D'avancer ... davantage ... Je sens le sommeil

Overpowers me ... | Qui me gagne ...

(aside, frightened)

Let me sleep ... never wake! | Un sommeil ... sans réveil!

(louder, in spite of herself)

I'm dying ... How I loved you! | J'étouffe! ... je succombe.

DES GRIEUX
(with animation and uneasiness)

Don't leave me now ... see the night is falling. | Reviens à toi! ... voici la nuit qui tombe!

There is the bright evening star! | C'est la première étoile! ...

MANON
(opening her eyes and looking at the sky with a smile)

Ah, what a pretty diamond! | Ah! le beau diamant!

(smiling)

You see, I'm still the same Manon. | Tu vois, je suis encore coquette!

DES GRIEUX
(gently)

Manon! Let's go! Manon! | On vient! ... Partons! Manon!

MANON
(with a dying voice)

I love you! | Je t'aime!

And with this kiss ... bid you farewell ... | Et ce baiser, c'est un adieu suprême!

(suffocating)

I love you! | Je t'aime!

DES GRIEUX
(in despair)

No! I will not believe it! Listen to me! | Non! ... je ne veux pas croire! Écoute-moi!

Do you recall? | Rappelle-toi!

Don't you feel my hand here on your hand pressing?	N'est-ce plus ma main que cette main presse?

MANON
(*vaguely*)

Ah, let me sleep in peace.	Ne me réveille pas!

DES GRIEUX

Don't you know my touch, tenderly caressing?	N'est-elle pour toi plus une caresse? ...

MANON

Ah, lift me in your arms!	Berce-moi dans tes bras!

DES GRIEUX

Do you know my voice even through my tears?	Reconnais ma voix à travers mes larmes!

MANON

We must forget the past!	Oublions le passé! ...

DES GRIEUX

You think I could forget you!	Souvenirs pleins de charmes! ...

MANON

Oh what have I done?	O cruels remords!

DES GRIEUX

I've forgiven you ...	Je t'ai pardonné!

MANON

How can I forget all I have done To spoil our love!	Ah! puis-je oublier les tristes jours De nos amours!

BOTH
[22]

Don't you ⎫ feel ⎰ my ⎱ hand here on Yes, I ⎭ ⎱ your ⎰ your ⎱ hand pressing ... my ⎰	N'est ce pas ma ⎫ main que cette main Oui, c'est bien sa ⎭ presse,
Ah, I turn and see!	N'est-ce pas ma ⎱ voix! Ah! c'est bien sa ⎰
Don't you ⎱ know ⎰ my ⎱ touch, tenderly Yes, I ⎰ ⎱ your ⎰ caressing	⎧ N'est-elle pour toi plus une caresse ⎩ Oui, c'est bien son cœur! c'est bien la tendresse
As it used to be!	⎧ Tout comme autrefois! ⎩ Des jours d'autrefois!
Let ⎱ our happy love ⎰ come ⎱ again! Soon ⎰ ⎱ will be born ⎰	Bientôt renaîtra le (bonheur) passé!

DES GRIEUX

All forgotten now!	Tout est oublié!

MANON
(*failing*)

Ah ... I'm dying. It must be. It must be!	Ah ... je meurs! ... Il le faut! C'est le pardon ...

DES GRIEUX
(*frightened*)

Manon!	Manon!

MANON
(murmuring)

Now you know the story Of Manon Lescaut!	Et c'est là l'histoire De Manon Lescaut!

She dies. With a heart-rending cry, Des Grieux falls on Manon's body.

Final Curtain.

Manon (Valerie Masterson) and Des Grieux (John Brecknock) in the last love duet on the road to Le Havre in the 1978 ENO production (photo: Andrew March)

Discgraphy *by Martin Hoyle*. For detailed analysis the enthusiast is referred to *Opera on Record*, ed. Alan Blyth (Hutchinson 1979). The recordings here listed are in French.

Conductor	*Plasson*	*Monteux*	*Rudel*
Orchestra/ Opera House	**Toulouse Capitole**	**Paris Opera-Comique**	**New Philharmonia**
Manon	Cotrubas	de los Angeles	Sills
Des Grieux	Kraus	Legay	Gedda
Lescaut	Quilico	Dens	Souzay
Comte des Grieux	van Dam	Borthayre	Bacquier
Disc UK number	EMI SLS1731413	HMV SLS5119	HMV SLS800
Tape UK number	TC-SLS1731413	TC-SLS5119	—
Disc US number	—	Seraphim 1D6057	ABC ATS 20007
Tape US number	—	—	5109-20007S

Selected excerpts

	Artists	Number
Adieu, notre petite table	Popp	4023326
Adieu, notre petite table	Callas	SXLP30166 TC-EXE74 (tape)
Je suis encore tout étourdie; Adieu, notre petite table; Suis-je gentille	Callas	2C165 54 178-88 (set of 11)
Adieu, notre petite table; Gavotte	de los Angeles	SLS5233 TC-SLS5233 (tape)
Instant charmant . . . En fermant les yeux	Gedda	SLS5250 TC-SLS5250 (tape)
Ah, fuyez, douce image	Domingo	SER5613

Bibliography

My Recollections, Massenet's more or less apocryphal memoirs, have been published in English (Greenwood Press, 1970).

The only biography of Massenet in English is by James Harding (Dent, 1970), which is sympathetic to the subject and entertaining. He is discussed in Martin Cooper's classic study *French Music from the Death of Berlioz to the Death of Fauré* (Oxford, 1951). The generation immediately before Massenet is the subject of T.J. Walsh's *Second Empire Opera* (Calder, 1981).

Prévost's novel has been translated several times, most recently by Richard Lesley (London, 1947) and L.W. Tancock (Penguin). In *Prévost: Manon Lescaut* (Arnold, 1976), Vivienne Mylne discusses the text for the purposes of students in French literature. Two general introductions to the literary background contain chapters of special interest: *The Evolution of the French Novel* by English Showalter (Princeton, 1972) and *The Eighteenth Century French Novel* by Vivienne Mylne (Cambridge, 1981).

Contributors

Gérard Condé is a regular contributor to musical journals and reviews and has researched extensively on Massenet.

Hugh Macdonald is Professor of Music at Glasgow University, the author of a study of Berlioz and the translator of a number of librettos for English National Opera.

Vivienne Mylne is Professor of French at the University of Kent at Canterbury, and specialises in 18th-century studies.

Edmund Tracey is Director of Drama and Text at English National Opera and has translated numerous operas.